Praise for

It's Not Like Being Black

"Riveting. From the opening paragraph of the introduction to the book's final page, *It's Not Like Being Black* is filled with common sense, uncommon insights, and sound biblical wisdom. Voddie Baucham is a refreshing voice of clarity, courage, and conviction in a morally insane culture now completely given over to irrationality and sexual perversion. He excels at tipping the sacred cows and debunking the mythology of the LGBTQ+ movement. 'Gay is not the new black,' he writes. 'It is merely the old sodomy.' Despite the difficulty of the subject matter, this is a remarkably well-written, timely, and edifying book."

—**John MacArthur**, pastor-teacher of Grace Community Church, chancellor of The Master's University and Seminary, and bestselling author

"Voddie Baucham is a trustworthy guide through the ever-changing cultural landscape of Western civilization. His biblical, theological, and historical analysis of the sexual anarchy through which we are living is both enlightening and convincing. He documents how sexual revolutionaries have purposefully and strategically worked to normalize what a few decades ago was universally recognized as perversion. One of their main tactics has been the co-opting of the language and good intentions of the civil rights movement. By marketing sexual perversions as 'like being black,' these cultural revolutionaries have successfully maneuvered themselves into positions of political power. This book explains their game plan and warns of what else is on their agenda.

"But Voddie is primarily a pastor. So he is not content simply to chart the methods and goals of the sexual revolution. He also shines the light of Scripture on the issues involved to help God's people navigate the turbulence being left in its wake. God's design for sexuality and marriage is clearly explained as being both right and good. And God's grace in Jesus Christ for both perpetrators and victims of sexual deviancy is pastorally commended to all who will look to Him in faith.

"This is a book that should be read by every pastor and church leader who wants to help people find the path of truth, joy, and hope in a world of sexual chaos. Young people who want to make sense of the sexually confused world in which they have grown up will find a wealth of biblical wisdom in these pages. I hope that it will be widely read."

—**Tom Ascol,** pastor of Grace Baptist Church
and president of Founders Ministries

"There are few issues in the Church today that are more of a threat to the gospel of Jesus Christ and His Church than the LGBTQIA+ movement. We need evangelical voices to speak to these issues with boldness, clarity, precision, and gospel hope. No one does this better than Voddie Baucham. Every Christian needs this book to understand the dangers of the LGBTQIA+ movement and to gain a thorough biblical response. Get it and read it today."

—**Tom Buck,** pastor of First Baptist Church in Lindale, Texas

"At last, the book that had to be written, and Voddie had to write it! I minister in post-apartheid South Africa, where civil rights and human dignity were cruelly disregarded for decades and continue to be today through reverse racism. Likewise, our African continent has known centuries of brutal enslavement along racial lines. What a colossal insult then to all these true victims of historic injustices to say that today's 'sexual minorities' are the oppressed ones. Voddie's book persuasively debunks that myth and dismantles that flawed argument with his characteristic clarity, thoroughness, and grace."

—**Tim Cantrell,** senior pastor of Antioch Bible Church and president of Shepherds' Seminary in Johannesburg, South Africa

"With the same scholarly research, biblical insight, and pastoral wisdom in which he masterfully exposed the belief system of Critical Race Theory in his bestselling book *Fault Lines*, Dr. Baucham uncovers the dark anti-God assumptions of the LGBTQIA+ movement in *It's Not Like Being Black*, powerfully equipping the Church with Scriptural weaponry that destroys the Serpent's arguments raised against the knowledge of God, for exclusive obedience to Christ. *It's Not Like Being Black* reveals that Satan's current crafty scheme is to use race as a trojan horse to bring in the gay and trans agenda, not only in society, but in the Church! I highly recommend this book to pastors who long for faithful boldness, to apologists who aspire for precision and persuasiveness, to evangelists and counselors for proclaiming liberty to the captives, to Seminary professors and their students for seeking preparation as the Lord's soldiers, and to all Christians who yearn to speak the truth in love."

—**Timothy Brindle,** associate pastor of Olive Street Presbyterian Church, senior stewardship officer at Westminster Theological Seminary, author, and Christian hip hop artist

"Dr. Voddie Baucham pulls no punches in his eye-opening exposé of the LGBTQ+ movement. *It's Not Like Being Black* teaches Christians the underlying logic and direction today's sexual revolutionaries are taking our country and churches. Every citizen should be concerned. From the civil rights era to the present, Dr. Baucham chronicles the way activists against the created order have used the path laid down by figures like MLK Jr. to promote their own nefarious intentions. While the book treats the damaging impact of degeneracy with honesty, it also offers hope for even the vilest of sinners with inspiring stories of redemption. Few men are as brave, humble, and honest as brother Baucham. This is a book you do not want to miss."

—**Jon Harris**, author, producer, cultural commentator, and host of the *Conversations That Matter* podcast

It's **Not** Like Being **Black**

It's **Not** Like Being **Black**

How Sexual Activists Hijacked the
Civil Rights Movement

Voddie T. Baucham Jr.

REGNERY
FAITH

Regnery Faith books may be purchased in bulk at special discounts for sales promotion, corporate gifts, fund-raising, or educational purposes. Special editions can also be created to specifications. For details, contact the Special Sales Department, Regnery Faith, 307 West 36th Street, 11th Floor, New York, NY 10018 or info@skyhorsepublishing.com.

Regnery Faith is an imprint of Skyhorse Publishing, Inc.®, a Delaware corporation.

Published in association with Yates & Yates, www.yates2.com.

Visit our website at www.regnery.com.

Please follow our publisher Tony Lyons on Instagram @tonylyonsisuncertain.

10 9 8 7 6 5 4 3 2

Library of Congress Cataloging-in-Publication Data is available on file.

Cover photo by Andrew Pearle Photography

Print ISBN: 978-1-68451-364-2
Ebook ISBN: 978-1-68451-437-3

Printed in the United States.

To the late Mwansa Mbewe (1991–2023), a student, friend, and dear brother whose short life left an indelible mark on all those with whom he came in contact. He was a gentle warrior who worked tirelessly to advance the Kingdom of Christ and bless his fellow man.

CONTENTS

Introduction: The Key to Pandora's Box   *ix*

SECTION ONE: THE MYTH OF THE "SEXUAL MINORITY"

Chapter 1:   The Making of the Myth   1

Chapter 2:   *Loving v. Virginia*   11

Chapter 3:   The Founders of the Feast   29

Chapter 4:   The Ubiquitous, Ever-Growing, Self-
Contradictory Acronym—Part I: LGBT   50

Chapter 5:   The Ubiquitous, Ever-Growing, Self-Contradictory
Acronym—Part II: QIA2S+   63

SECTION TWO: THE GROWTH OF THE MOVEMENT

Chapter 6:   How We Got Here   83

Chapter 7:   The Enemy Within   97

SECTION THREE: THE TRUTH WE MUST DEFINE AND DEFEND

Chapter 8:   Is It Fair to Use the Bible?   121

Chapter 9:   What Happens When We Buy the Lie?   140

Chapter 10: God's Design for Marriage   158

Chapter 11: And Such Were Some of You   178

Conclusion   *195*

Endnotes   *206*

The worst part of all of this is the fact that, in our upside-down world, if you see anything wrong with all of this, you're

The Key to Pandora's Box

We are living in crazy times. Biological men are competing and winning against biological women in high school,[1] college,[2] professional sports,[3] and the Olympics.[4] We are constantly warned about the dangers of toxic masculinity, but when a biological male MMA fighter fractured the orbital bone of a biological female during an officially sanctioned event,[5] we responded with a wink and a nod because he identified as a woman. And to add insult to injury, there have even been trans contestants crowned in beauty contests![6] Not only can the newest justice on the U.S. Supreme Court not answer the simple question "What is a woman?"[7] but neither can college professors, doctors, or psychologists who are deemed to be at the top of their field.[8] In fact, it's gotten so weird that now state governments are being forced to define the word, as Oklahoma governor Kevin Stitt did in August 2023 through an executive order.[9]

The worst part of all of this is the fact that, in our upside-down world, if you see anything wrong with all of this, *you're* the crazy one! If you doubt that men can become pregnant, some women have penises, and infants suffer from gender dysphoria, you're the uneducated, simple-minded, evil, and dangerous one whom society needs to fear.

You may think all of this happened overnight. I assure you, it didn't. What we are witnessing now is the result of a long series of ideological shifts, court decisions, political maneuvers, and educational strategies whose aims still have yet to be fully realized. And at the heart of much of the change is the idea that the battle for the rights of so-called "sexual minorities" is the latest front in America's civil rights struggle, stemming from a single lie that took root in our culture: "Sexual orientation is no different than race."

This lie came to a head in 2015, when the U.S. Supreme Court handed down its decision in *Obergefell v. Hodges*—the case that overrode every existing state law and constitutional amendment defining marriage as the union of one man and one woman. Associate Justice Anthony Kennedy penned the majority opinion in the landmark decision heralded by gay activists from coast to coast, writing that:

> The Constitution promises liberty to all within its reach, a liberty that includes certain specific rights that allow persons, within a lawful realm, to *define and express their identity*. The petitioners in these cases seek to find that liberty by marrying someone of the same sex and having their marriages deemed lawful on the same terms and conditions as marriages between persons of the opposite sex.[10] (emphasis mine)

While many Christians and political conservatives saw *Obergefell* as the end game in the leftists' agenda, activists saw it as a stepping stone.

It is no coincidence that we have witnessed a proliferation in issues related to sexual minorities since *Obergefell*. Whether it's the explosion of transgenderism, the proliferation of sexually explicit materials in schools, drag queen story hour, rebranding pedophiles as "minor-attracted persons" and the attending push to include them in the "sexual minority" group, or the introduction of such outlandish identities as "furries," the post-*Obergefell* landscape has produced a dizzying array of people taking Kennedy up on his suggestion to "define and express their identity."

For those of us who follow Christ, the moral decay is more than enough to cause alarm. However, there is a more pressing issue at hand: *Obergefell* set the stage for new "tension in the debate regarding sexual orientation anti-discrimination and religious freedom."[11] What this looks like, argues University of Massachusetts law professor Jeremiah Ho, is a battle between "the autonomy of sexual minorities to be who and what they are, and the autonomy of those whose religious beliefs may not have accepting views of sexual minorities being who they are."[12] And that battle has already begun in earnest.

In a June 2023 report to the UN Human Rights Council, Victor Madrigal-Borloz, a Costa Rican attorney who at press time was in residence at the Harvard University Law School, recommended that the United States "refrain from justifying with religious narratives any act of violence and discrimination based on sexual orientation and gender identity."[13] That means no one can use or quote from the Bible to address sexual sin. Madrigal-Borloz went on to add that government authorities should "prevent and investigate such acts and ensure the accountability of perpetrators and the provision of effective remedies for damages."[14]

This is dangerous rhetoric! This is a declaration of war on the God of the Bible and all those who worship Him. "He who justifies the wicked and he who condemns the righteous are both alike an abomination to the LORD" (Proverbs 17:15).

If we buy the lie that sexual proclivities and preferences are equivalent to race; if we believe that the fight for the rights of "sexual minorities" is the final frontier in the struggle for civil rights, we are not only opening Pandora's box, but are insulting whole swaths of people who have fought legitimate civil rights struggles.

I am a black man, a descendant of slaves. I was born in South Los Angeles and have spent the last eight years living and serving in Africa. Anyone looking at me can see that I am black. I don't "define and express my identity" as black. I was born black, and I will die black. So allow me to state one thing here that we'll spend the rest of this book unpacking:

Whether you identify as gay, lesbian, bisexual, transgender, trigender, multigender, two-spirit, furry, queer, demiflux, otherkin, or as a mermaid, a British Columbian wolf, or an avian-human hybrid:[15]

Not one of those things is like being black.

SECTION ONE

The Myth of the "Sexual Minority"

CHAPTER I

The Making of the Myth

In December 2008, America's leading gay magazine, *The Advocate*, ran a cover article under the headline "Gay Is the New Black." The author, responding to California voters' decision to continue defining marriage as the union of one man and one woman, wrote:

> It's impossible not to imagine what might have happened
> if the civil rights of African Americans, Hispanics, women,
> or any other minority had been reversed by public refer-
> endum. If any other group of people in America had their
> fundamental rights subjected to popular vote, there would
> be universal outrage in this country.[1]

The idea that the battle over same-sex marriage was a continu-
ation of the civil rights battles of the 1960s was both strategic
and ubiquitous at the time. Gay activists had made a concerted
effort to burn this idea into the collective conscience of America

decades earlier, and it had worked. The idea that homosexuality was equivalent to race had caught on.

To be fair, even the proponents of this argument knew it was a stretch. The author of *The Advocate* article admitted,

> Our oppression . . . is nowhere near as extreme as blacks', and we insult them when we make facile comparisons between our plights. . . . Gay people have more resources than blacks had in the 1960s.[2]

But the strength of the gay-equals-black argument lies not in the accuracy of its comparison but in the effectiveness of its propaganda. And that has never been clearer than it became in the summer of 2015.

A Tale of Two Stories

In July 2015, two seemingly unrelated stories highlighted the effectiveness of this propaganda. The first was when the U.S. Supreme Court declared same-sex "marriage" a constitutional right. The second was a story from the other side of the country: Rachel Dolezal, the leader of the NAACP chapter in Spokane, Washington, made headlines when people discovered she was a white woman who had been pretending to be black for many years.

What do these two events have to do with each other?

Dolezal was doing the same thing the LGBTQIA+ lobby, led by lesbians and gay men, had been doing for years: She was working to leverage political power by pretending to be part of an aggrieved minority group. And, like those who identify as homosexuals, her identification was rooted in a history of deep personal feelings and a lifestyle based on living in accordance with those feelings.

"I definitely am not white," she declared on NBC News, noting that by the age of five, she

> was drawing self-portraits with the brown crayon instead of the peach crayon, and black curly hair. . . . Nothing about being white describes who I am. . . . The closest thing that I can come to is if—if you're black or white, I'm black. I'm more black than I am white.[3]

This sounds exactly like the testimony of people who declare themselves to be "sexual minorities." They've "known" it since they were children. They've acted upon that knowledge, built their lives around that identity, and presented themselves to the world in that way.

I can already hear the objections to this comparison. "But being black is based on genetics." Right—and so is being male or female, but that hasn't stopped us from declaring lately that "trans women are women." We allow transsexuals to use bathrooms and even compete in the Olympics based on their biology-contradicting self-declarations. And we declare homosexuality to be as innate and immutable as ethnicity despite a complete absence of any biological evidence for that belief. This is all because we are dealing not with facts, but with propaganda.

Consider what Kennedy wrote in *Obergefell*.

> Far from seeking to devalue marriage, the petitioners seek it for themselves because of their respect and need for its *privileges and responsibilities*. And their immutable nature

dictates that same-sex marriage is their only real path to this profound commitment.[4] (emphasis mine)

Kennedy identified homosexuality as having an "immutable nature," skipping right over the argument that it is genetically determined—a highly debatable claim at best—to the idea that it cannot be changed. He offered no evidence for his assertion because there is none. In fact, there is quite a lot of evidence to the contrary.

The U.S. Centers for Disease Control and Prevention (CDC) defines sexual orientation as "a person's sexual and emotional attraction to another person and the behavior and/or social affiliation that may result from this attraction."[5] According to the Association of Cognitive and Behavioral Therapies, sexual orientation has at least three components: 1) the type of person to whom someone is romantically and/or sexually attracted (i.e., attractions); 2) the type of person with whom someone has sex (i.e., behavior); and 3) how someone labels or identifies himself (i.e., identity).[6] I share these two definitions because they are consistent with other mainstream definitions that make no mention of the "identities" of "sexual minorities" being either innate or immutable. According to these definitions, the only things that matter are what you desire, what you do, and what you declare—the same standards Dolezal used to justify her identity as a black woman even though she was clearly not one.

These two stories continue to bear their contradictory witness. One proclaims that you are what you declare you are (and how you choose to live), and that the law must respect and reflect that choice. The other proclaims that you have no right to declare yourself to be a member of a minority group without sufficient biological evidence to back up that claim. Ironically, Rachel Dolezal is more like me ethnically than she ever will be in terms of her gender since the distance between black people and white people is a matter of degree, while male and female are entirely separate categories.

So why do we play these games? Because of a well-placed myth.

The Myth of the Sexual Minority

The notion of so-called "sexual minorities" is a myth. According to the Association for Behavioral and Cognitive Therapies, this is "an umbrella term used to refer to anyone who is not heterosexual or straight."[7] The CDC defines sexual minorities as individuals "who *identify* as gay, lesbian, or bisexual, or who are attracted to or have sexual contact with people of the same gender."[8] In other words, these are people with rare, unnatural proclivities that used to be deemed sinful, but have now gained acceptance.

This raises at least two important questions. First, why use the term "minorities"? And second, why exclude other people whose sexual proclivities fall outside accepted sexual boundaries? The answers to these two questions reveal the truth behind the label.

To answer the first question, let's look instances where we don't use the term "minorities." Somewhere around 5 percent of college students major in engineering,[9] but we would never refer to those people as "academic minorities." Why? Because the term has a special connotation in contemporary culture. It is not a mathematical term, but a political and philosophical one. For example, even though most undergraduate university degrees are granted to female students,[10] no one would refer to men as "academic minorities"—but we refer to women not only in academic but professional settings as minorities even though there are more of them, and have been throughout recent history.[11] Again, the term "minority" has little to do with mathematics.

When progressives use that word, they are usually referring to people who are not part of the hegemonic power structure. The assumption is that white, male, heterosexual, cisgendered, able-bodied, native-born Christians are in the driver's seat and everyone else is an oppressed minority. But that still leaves our second question: Why leave other sexual proclivities, such as pedophiles or zoophiles, off the list?

The answer is simply that those types of deviance have not yet gained the cultural acceptance of homosexuality, bisexuality, or transgenderism. But make no mistake: There is a playbook, which we will discuss in more detail in later chapters, and the progressive lobby is working methodically through it not only to normalize all these things, but to protect them through the force of law.

The sexual minority myth is rooted in neo-Marxist critical theory assumptions about hegemony. For the Critical Theorist, the traditions of Western civilization in general, and Christianity in particular, are neither true and beautiful, nor good; they simply hold sway because of their position of hegemonic dominance. To the intersectional Critical Theorist, ideas like cis-heteronormativity are mere inventions designed to favor and empower certain groups and individuals and allow them to oppress others. The question is not "What hath God said?" because in their minds, there is no God to speak—just men who seek power. Thus, there is no right or wrong, only oppressors and the oppressed. And in the case of human sexuality, the oppressors are those who have imposed standards of Christian morality in order to oppress those who find themselves in the "minority."

This is an important point to grasp for those trying to make sense of the current moral and political climate. We must recognize that we are in the midst of a battle over the very source and nature of truth. That is why cultural elites tell us to "trust the science" while simultaneously telling us that NCAA swimming champ Lia Thomas is a woman and men can menstruate. Remember, for the Critical Theorist, even knowledge is "socially constructed," so there can be no universal moral standards. Therefore, transgenderism is not "wrong," it's just marginalized in a culture that has *centered* the cisgender identity. Homosexuality is not sinful; it is simply a minority behavior in a heteronormative society.

Kennedy's argument is a classic example of the "sexual minority" ideology at work. He views homosexuals as an identifiable minority that has been denied certain rights. The first clue to his underlying worldview is the fact that his argument is rooted in question-begging assumptions about sexual orientation. As stated earlier, he views sexual orientation as "immutable." This position has far less to do with science than it does with philosophy.

The majority opinion Kennedy wrote also equates "desire" with "rights" by arguing that "the petitioners seek (marriage)," and should have it granted to them "because of their respect and *need*" for it. The decision also reduces marriage to a set of "privileges and responsibilities" granted by the state instead of an institution created by God that the state privileges as a way of acknowledging its unique, God-given nature.

The Consequences

Obergefell has far-reaching consequences. The standardization of same-sex marriage overturned thousands of years of human history and tradition, threatened the fabric of Western civilization, and laid the groundwork for the persecution of Christians.

Even Kennedy acknowledged this major departure from history when he wrote:

> From their beginning to their most recent page, the annals of human history reveal the transcendent importance of marriage. . . . The lifelong union of a man and a woman always has promised nobility and dignity to all persons, without regard to their station in life. . . . Marriage is sacred to those who live by their religions and offers unique fulfillment to those who find meaning in the secular realm.[12]

But departing from history is not inherently wrong. The very existence of the United States testifies to that fact, as do the abolition of slavery, women's suffrage, and overturning *Plessy v. Ferguson* and *Roe v. Wade*. In many ways, history is only a collection of a series of changes that take place over time. However, there are some things that don't change, or do so only slightly and rarely—and marriage is one of those things. It is a foundational institution that has defined and distinguished humanity across all cultures. There have been changes to its structure (i.e., arranged marriages, dowry, polygamy, etc.), but not to its essence. At its core, marriage has always united men and women.

Same-sex marriage, therefore, has threatened Western civilization. I don't mean that issuing marriage licenses to same-sex couples, in itself, will destroy Western civilization, but rather that the assumptions underlying *Obergefell* are rooted in a worldview that is contrary to that which sustains Western civilization.[13]

As an American, I never really thought about our biblical, theological, and philosophical heritage. As a black American, all I was ever encouraged to think of in that regard was America's heritage of slavery and injustice. However, leaving America (and the West) by moving my family to Zambia several years ago has allowed me to look at Western civilization with new eyes and great appreciation. It has also caused me great alarm as I have watched the cult of sexual minorities hijack the legitimate grievances of the civil rights movement in ways that undermine the very foundations upon which Western civilization is built.

Since historic Christianity and its resulting worldview serve as the foundation upon which Western civilization is built, any attempt to rewrite or overthrow Western civilization must necessarily include efforts to rewrite and/or overthrow historic Christianity. And this is exactly what we have seen both in the days leading up to *Obergefell* and after.

From the Fringe to the Forefront

The process of turning sinners into sexual minorities didn't happen overnight. It was slow, calculated, and methodical. There were five ideological steps in the process:

Step One: Change the name of the sin (for instance, "sodomy" became "homosexuality" and is now "gay"; efforts currently are underway to change the terms "pedophile" and "pederast" to "minor-attracted person").

Step Two: Transform the behavior from a sin to an identity.
Step Three: Juxtapose that identity with the civil rights struggle of black people and other minorities.
Step Four: Replace the Christianity of the Bible with an apostate version that picks and chooses rites, rituals, and morals to suit the new regime.
Step Five: Pretend to be surprised when other groups use the same tactics to try to normalize the unimaginable.

Make no mistake about it; other "identities" are now traveling the same well-worn paths that led to *Obergefell*. Polygamists, polyamorists, and pedophiles have already staked their claims.

To sum up: Gay is not the new black; it is merely the old sodomy. And standardizing the recognition of same-sex "marriage" is nothing at all like doing away with the antimiscegenation laws that once prevented black people from marrying white people. We'll talk about that in the next chapter.

CHAPTER 2

Loving v. Virginia

I am not a big selfie guy. However, there are times when even I feel the need to grab my phone and snap a pic. One such moment happened several years ago when I was preaching at a church in Georgia. Afterward, a woman told me she was a direct descendant of Pocahontas and the English settler John Rolfe. The homeschooling dad and history buff in me leapt to the surface, and all I could think was, "Wait till I tell the kids!" My family and I have always been fascinated by the story of Pocahontas.

In May 1607, about one hundred English colonists settled along the James River in Virginia, establishing Jamestown as the first English settlement in America. Its early days were marked by famine, disease, and attacks by natives, mostly from the local Powhatan tribe. Nevertheless, the settlers survived, mainly due to the efforts of twenty-seven-year-old adventurer John Smith.

In December 1607, Smith and two other colonists were captured by Powhatan warriors. His two companions were killed, but Smith was spared and released. According to his personal account, that was due to intervention from Chief Wahunsonacock's thirteen-year-old daughter, Matoaka (whom we know by her nickname, Pocahontas). Because of this well-known historical event, many mistakenly believe that Pocahontas married John Smith.

In early 1613, the English kidnapped Pocahontas, then nineteen, in the hopes of using her to negotiate peace with her father. They put her in the custody of Sir Thomas Gates, the marshal of Virginia. While in his household, Pocahontas (who was reportedly treated as a guest during the negotiations) converted to Christianity and was baptized. Upon her baptism, she became known as Lady Rebecca. By the time her father had agreed to the terms of her release, she had fallen in love with tobacco farmer John Rolfe, a white settler.

The two were married on April 5, 1613, with the blessing of both Chief Wahunsonacock and the governor of Virginia. In 1616, Pocahontas (affectionately known as "the Indian Princess") and Rolfe sailed to England, where she was presented at the court of King James I. Pocahontas died of smallpox in 1617 at the age of twenty-three, a day before she and Rolfe were scheduled to sail back to Virginia.

I mention this story because of its stark contrast with another interracial marriage that took place in the same locale some three and a half centuries later.

Antimiscegenation

In June 1958, Mildred Jeter (a black woman) and Richard Loving (a white man) were married in Washington, D.C. Shortly afterward, they settled in Caroline County, Virginia. In October 1958, a grand jury of the Circuit Court of Caroline County charged the Lovings with violating the state ban on interracial marriage, which had been in place since 1924. On January 6, 1959, the Lovings pled guilty to the charge and were sentenced to one year in jail apiece. The trial judge suspended the sentence for a period of twenty-five years on the condition that the Lovings leave Virginia and not return together for that time period.

This case is one of the most poignant reminders of America's racist past. It has also come to symbolize the fight for so-called "marriage equality."

The main argument goes like this: "Christianity/The Church is wrong on same-sex marriage the same way it was wrong on interracial marriage—and just like then, religious bigots need to catch up with the times." It sounds straightforward, but I assure you it is not. The analogy is flawed, the logic is tortured, and the underlying consequences are now upon us like a crouching lion that has been waiting to pounce on his unsuspecting prey. You see, if sexual orientation is analogous to race, and it is both immoral and illegal to deny people marriage based on race, then the current "religious exemptions" that accompany measures like the ironically titled "Respect for Marriage Act" that Congress passed in 2022 are temporary placeholders that must eventually give way; the LGBTQ lobby has given full throat, both historically and recently, to its intent to demolish opposition to its agenda by silencing biblical Christians entirely. With that in mind, let's examine the argument more closely.

The trial judge in *Loving* stated:

Almighty God created the races white, black, yellow, malay and red, and he placed them on separate continents.

And but for the interference with his arrangement there would be no cause for such marriages. The fact that he separated the races shows that he did not intend for the races to mix.[1]

This kind of thinking would be comical if it weren't so offensive, and if it hadn't left such a track record of brutality and inhumanity in its wake. However, is it fair to lay this thinking at the feet of Christendom? Especially in light of the fact that Pocahontas and John Rolfe were married in a Christian ceremony in colonial Virginia three and a half centuries earlier?

The common refrain from critical and post-colonial theorists is that America was and is uniquely racist, and that racism was and is uniquely Christian. Remember the oppression matrix: At the core of the hegemonic power that oppresses minorities in America is the white, male, heterosexual, cisgendered, native-born Christian. And, according to the newly popular revisionism that traces America's founding to 1619—the year the first African slaves arrived on shore—rather than our liberation from Britain in 1776, slavery is the *sine qua non* of America's racist history. However, this ideology ignores several important historical facts that are relevant to *Loving*.

First, slavery is not uniquely American. It has existed in every corner of the globe, and in every era, including the modern one. Today there are between twenty-five million and forty million slaves in the world.[2] (In fact, the word "slave" itself comes from the word "Slav," referring to the Slavic peoples of eastern Europe.)[3] The Bible is replete with ancient examples of slavery, as are myriad ancient texts. Slavery is as old as humanity and thus could not possibly be uniquely American.

LOVING V. VIRGINIA   15

Second, as Thomas Sowell has aptly noted, "Slavery was not based on race, much less on theories about race."[4] This is why

> before the modern era, by and large Europeans enslaved other Europeans, Asians enslaved other Asians, Africans enslaved other Africans, and the indigenous peoples of the Western Hemisphere enslaved other indigenous peoples of the Western Hemisphere.[5]

Modern theories about race were a product, not the cause, of slavery. "Only relatively late in history," notes Sowell, "did enslavement across racial lines occur on such a scale as to promote an ideology of racism that outlasted the institution of slavery itself."[6]

What was unique about American slavery was not the fact that it existed, but that it met moral opposition (by the Christian abolitionist movement) and ended within a century after America's founding. In fact, Sowell notes, "only one civilization developed a moral revulsion against [slavery], very late in its history—Western civilization."[7] And the main impetus for that was Christianity.

So why did Virginia and neighboring states have laws allowing chattel slavery?

"Only in the American South did a large apologetic literature develop, seeking to justify slavery," notes Sowell, "because only there was slavery under such large-scale and sustained attacks on moral grounds as to require a response."[8]

America was (and is) the land rooted in the principles of the Declaration of Independence, where "all men are created equal." Thus, Sowell explains, "the only way to justify slavery was by depicting those enslaved as not fully men." Consequently, a particularly virulent form of racism thus arose from a particularly desperate need to defend slavery against telling attacks that invoked the fundamental principles of the American republic. Nowhere else in the world was slavery in such dire straits ideologically and nowhere else did racism reach such heights (or depths) in defense of the institution.[9]

That defense of slavery gave rise to a uniquely pernicious form of racism. Again, Sowell's insight is informative:

racism was neither necessary nor sufficient for slavery, whose origins antedated racism by centuries. Racism was a result, not a cause, of slavery and not all societies that enslaved people of another race became pervaded with racism to the extent that the American South did.[10]

In *Loving v. Virginia*, the U.S. Supreme Court acknowledged the link between slavery and antimiscegenation, noting, "Penalties for miscegenation arose as an incident to slavery and have been common in Virginia since the colonial period."[11] It is impossible to understand *Loving* without taking this historical background into account.

The Loving Fight

After their convictions, the Lovings relocated to the District of Columbia, where interracial marriage was not banned. On November 6, 1963, they filed a motion to vacate the state's judgment and set aside their sentences on the ground that the statute they had violated was "repugnant to the Fourteenth Amendment."[12] A year later, their motion had yet to be decided, so the Lovings filed a class-action lawsuit in the District Court for the Eastern District of Virginia requesting that a three-judge panel be convened to declare the Virginia antimiscegenation statute unconstitutional. This would also prevent the state from enforcing their convictions.

On January 22, 1965, the state trial judge denied the motion to vacate the Lovings' sentences. The couple then appealed to the state appellate court. On February 11, 1965, a three-judge panel allowed the Lovings to present their constitutional claims to the Virginia Supreme Court, [13] saying,

> the State argues that the meaning of the Equal Protection Clause, as illuminated by the statements of the Framers, is only that state penal laws containing an interracial element as part of the definition of the offense must apply equally to whites and Negroes in the sense that members of each race are punished to the same degree. Thus, the State contends that, because its miscegenation statutes punish equally both the white and the Negro participants in an interracial marriage, these statutes, despite their reliance on racial classifications, do not constitute an invidious discrimination based upon race.[14]

Section 20–59 stated that violating the law was a felony punishable by up to five years in prison.[15]

When *Loving* reached the U.S. Supreme Court, the justices rightly and definitively struck down Virginia's egregious marriage law, writing:

> Marriage is one of the "basic civil rights of man," fundamental to our very existence and survival. *Skinner v.*

Oklahoma, 316 U. S. 535, 541 (1942). See also *Maynard v. Hill*, 125 U. S. 190 (1888). To deny this fundamental freedom on so unsupportable a basis as the racial classifications embodied in these statutes, classifications so directly subversive of the principle of equality at the heart of the Fourteenth Amendment, is surely to deprive all the State's citizens of liberty without due process of law. The Fourteenth Amendment requires that the freedom of choice to marry not be restricted by invidious racial discriminations. Under our Constitution, the freedom to marry, or not marry, a person of another race resides with the individual and cannot be infringed by the State. . . . These convictions must be reversed. . . . It is so ordered.[16]

With that, one of the darkest chapters of America's racist past came to a close.

For some, though, this ruling was merely a prelude to what they now see as the next phase of the struggle regarding LGBTQIA+ "rights." But are they correct? Should we view those issues through the lens of *Loving v. Virginia*? Or is it possible that both the Virginia antimiscegenation statute and the LGBTQIA+ lobby are wrong?

Why Two Wrongs Can Both Be Wrong

The LGBTQIA+ crowd landed on a winning argument with the "sexual orientation equals race" mantra. It allowed them to hitch their wagons to *Loving* and put conservatives and Christians on defense.

On its face, that argument seems to make sense. Antimiscegenation laws discriminated against people by forbidding them to marry based on race (an immutable characteristic).[17] Marriage laws historically have discriminated against people by forbidding them to marry based on sexual orientation (also deemed to be an immutable characteristic).

This argument, as we know, won the day. The law of the land now includes same-sex marriage. This argument is also important because it acknowledges the legal and moral nature of marriage. I've said this before, and I will say it again: Those who push back against Christians for making moral arguments for marriage are hypocrites. There is no other way to look at marriage; it is inherently both a legal and a moral issue.

With that in mind, let's look at the specific legal and moral issues that separate *Loving* and same-sex marriage—again with the understanding that *Obergefell* paved the way for all the cultural madness we are currently experiencing and that which is still waiting in the wings for its moment in the spotlight.

Virginia Violated the Definition of Marriage

Central to the argument of this book is the fact that humans do not get to define marriage. Nor do governments define marriage; they merely *acknowledge* the definition of marriage. God alone gets to define marriage. In *Loving*, the U.S. Supreme Court noted:

> The central features of this Act, and current Virginia law, are the absolute prohibition of a "white person" marrying other than another "white person," a prohibition against issuing marriage licenses until the issuing official is satisfied that the applicants' statements as to their race are correct, certificates of "racial composition" to be kept by

both local and state registrars, and the carrying forward of earlier prohibitions against racial intermarriage.[18]

Virginia added the dimension of race to the definition of marriage, which has never been supported biblically. For example, Judah's marriage to a Canaanite, Moses's marriage to a Midianite, Boaz's marriage to a Moabite, and John Rolfe's marriage to Pocahontas all point to interethnic marriage as an historical norm. Antimiscegenation laws were anomalies, and history is replete with examples that prove this fact. Hence, Virginia's antimiscegenation law redefined marriage—which, ironically, means those who used *Loving* as a pretext for supporting same-sex marriage were in fact arguing for the very thing that made the Virginia law untenable.

Virginia's Law Was Established for the Purpose of Discrimination

The Virginia antimiscegenation law not only violated the definition of marriage, it did so for expressly racist reasons. It was part of the Racial Integrity Act of 1924, passed during a period of "extreme nativism" at the end of WWI.[19] As the U.S. Supreme Court noted,

the state court concluded that the State's legitimate purposes were "to preserve the racial integrity of its citizens," and to prevent "the corruption of blood," "a mongrel breed of citizens," and "the obliteration of racial pride," obviously an endorsement of the doctrine of White Supremacy.[20]

The evidence of this racist and discriminatory practice is seen in the fact that it was applied exclusively to marriages involving white people:

> There is patently no legitimate overriding purpose independent of invidious racial discrimination which justifies this classification. The fact that Virginia prohibits only interracial marriages involving white persons demonstrates that the racial classifications must stand on their own justification, as measures designed to maintain White Supremacy.[21]

So people of color could marry anyone other than white people, but white people could only marry each other. This could not have been more blatant. Nor could it have been more heinous.

The only way this could be equated with same-sex marriage is if state or federal laws had been rewritten with the express purpose of eliminating homosexual practices. Moreover, in light of the previous point, the practices would have to have been in place since the beginning of time. As such, same-sex marriage was an inconceivable notion until very recently. How, then, could existing marriage law discriminate against it?

Let me illustrate this with a couple of personal examples from back in the day.

Me and Senator Ellis

In the summer of 2006, the Texas Senate was debating whether to allow the citizens of the state to vote on an amendment to the state constitution defining marriage. There was no question such an amendment would pass. The homosexual lobby's only hope was killing the bill in the Senate subcommittee where it was then being debated. Normally, this would not have been an issue. Texas is a very conservative state, and the bill had popular support. However, one of the members of the committee was Senator Rodney Ellis, a powerful black legislator from the Houston area. Not only was he only playing the race card on this issue, he was playing it from the bottom of the deck—basing his opposition to the bill on the notion that same-sex marriage was a civil rights issue.

The Texas State Capitol is one of the most impressive in the nation. As I pulled into the parking lot, I could not help but be intimidated. That intimidation only grew as I approached the Senate chamber. While I waited to be called, I sat through hours of testimony from other witnesses, the overwhelming majority of which favored same-sex marriage. In fact, I only remember hearing from one other person from the conservative side. I was also struck by the fact that none of the people who testified faced any questions or rebuttal, which came as a great relief. I had preached in front of tens of thousands of people before, but the idea of being grilled by a group of state senators in front of a packed chamber was more than a little unsettling. This was not my wheelhouse.

When I was called, I sensed that this would be a defining moment, and indeed it was. Most of the people there were students and faculty from the University of Texas, just up the road. Almost all of them represented the pro-same-sex-marriage side. There were also several clergy in the room, most of whom also were pro-same-sex marriage. Then there was the press, which was undoubtedly pro-same-sex marriage. As I walked through the crowd to take my place at the microphone, many in the crowd nodded and smiled at me. Those people saw my skin color, heard me introduced as "reverend" (I have never liked that), and assumed I would be joining the chorus of voices calling upon the committee to refuse to let the bill come before the people of Texas for a vote.

I thanked the senators for the opportunity to address them, then laid out my argument for a constitutional amendment affirming the definition of marriage as a union between a man and a woman. I refuted the idea that gay is the new black, or that same-sex marriage was a civil rights issue.

As I spoke, I could feel the air leaving the room. The smiles turned to scornful glares, and the nods of approval transformed into heads shaking in bewilderment. Yet the room was so silent you could hear a pen drop. I also noticed that the senators, most of whom had been leaning back, talking to aides, or shuffling papers during most of the testimony, were suddenly on the edges of their seats.

When I finished my remarks, I thanked the senators, gathered my notes, and prepared to leave, just like everyone who had testified before me. But something was different. As soon as I finished speaking, all the senators on the committee turned and looked in the same direction—at Senator Rodney Ellis, the man who was holding the bill hostage. What happened next changed the tone of the entire proceeding, as Ellis and I squared off. The debate didn't last long, maybe a few minutes. However, its impact was significant.

As the senators fixed their gaze on him as if to say, "What are you going to do with this guy?" Ellis sat up in his chair and did what no one else had done: He asked me a question.

"What personal experience do you have in the civil rights movement?"[22]

The question was calculated. I was in my thirties at the time, and therefore too young to have been involved in the civil rights movement of the 1960s, and Ellis knew that. Second, he was a senator from Houston who knew I was a pastor serving in the area; if I had been involved in more recent civil rights issues, he would have known about it. Also, I was speaking against same-sex marriage, and there were few civil rights-minded black pastors doing that. Thus, with a single question, Ellis hoped to discredit me by painting me as a young black conservative who was out of touch with the civil rights struggles of his own people.

However, I had just spent two hours in the car prepping for such a question, and fired back. I alluded to the 70 percent out-of-wedlock birthrate among black Americans and noted that fatherlessness is the greatest blight on the black community. I noted that I was not only a father, but also an adoptive father who was committed to doing more than marching on behalf of theoretical people in need; I was giving my very life to actual people in need. Ellis backed off of that line of questioning immediately.

He asked me a couple more questions, then stopped when he realized I used each one to point to more facts about how homosexuality is not like being black and why Texas needed to preserve the definition of marriage in the state constitution.

Then another strange thing happened: A second member of the committee leaned forward and asked me something to the effect of, "If we allow this bill to get out of our committee, do you think the other side should agree to . . ." I was completely lost! I shrugged my shoulders and said, "Senator, I have no idea." Then the legislators began to converse with one another, and I was dismissed.

As I turned and walked away, I couldn't help but feel like a cross between Daniel in the lions' den and the Christians in the Colosseum. I am a big man, and not easily intimidated by hostile crowds. But at that moment, all I could think was, *Maybe I should have brought security.* As I was leaving the room, a man who identified himself as an aide to one of the senators reached out, shook my hand, then leaned in to whisper in my ear, "I don't agree with your position on this, but you just ended this debate." That bill went on pass the committee, then the Senate and the House. Eventually, it was passed overwhelmingly by the people of Texas.

But when the U.S. Supreme Court ruled on *Obergefell* nine years later, that constitutional amendment was rendered meaningless. Nonetheless, there are three important lessons we should learn from this.

The first is that the changes we have seen in state and federal law, as well as our culture, are not based on scientific facts, but on political maneuvering and the manipulation of public opinion. When Senator Ellis came at me with what amounted to an *ad hominem* attack, he revealed the lack of substance in his position. He didn't come at me with the latest scientific findings; he called my black card. His actions said to everyone involved, "This is a question of minority status and grievance. Nothing more."

The second lesson is that the political maneuvering and manipulation of public opinion is vulnerable to frontal assault. When I, as a black man, stood up and challenged the narrative, I became a threat. That's why I was treated differently than all the other witnesses; I had to be dealt with. I had to be discredited. The other people in the room could not be allowed to understand that there is not a single, unassailable "minority" perspective on civil rights and homosexuality—or anything else. To do so would remove the unseen yet palpable veil of protection Ellis and his colleagues enjoyed and invite actual debate. As things stood, all opposition could be dismissed as "homophobia" from powerful, insensitive members of the hegemonic elite trying to maintain their power.

The last lesson is that it doesn't take much to expose the lie and flip the script. That is why progressives engage in the politics of character assassination. They can't win based on the merits of their arguments, so they engage in vicious, emotional, manipulative tactics. That's why conservatives and Christians can't just be wrong on the issues; we have to be "homophobes." We can't just have a difference of opinion, we have to be guilty of "spreading hate."

If we are wrong, they have to demonstrate that with facts. If we have a difference of opinion, they have to argue the merits of their case. And that is exactly what they don't want to do. They would prefer to gently lay the race card on the table and watch their opponents squirm.

Not the Same Thing by a Long Shot!

The "gay equals black" argument relies on a number of flawed presuppositions, chiefly the idea that all discrimination is bad. Nothing could be further from the case: *All* laws are discriminatory in some way. Laws against speeding discriminate against those who drive too fast. Laws requiring electric vehicles discriminate against vehicles that use gas. Laws against murder discriminate against those who, well, murder. And marriage laws are no different. Laws that prevent people who are already married, people who are too young, or people who are too closely related from getting married are all discriminatory in some way.

The problem is not discrimination. Our problem is always the standard upon which the discrimination is based.

In *Loving*, the discrimination was based on race; something that had never been part of the definition of marriage—but sex (as in male and female) has always been part of the definition of marriage. As I mentioned previously, race and sex are not remotely the same thing. Beyond that, discrimination based on race or ethnicity is completely counter to the biblical foundation upon which our ethics and morals are built. This was the clarion call of the Civil Rights movement, which was led largely by black Christians. Black people held up the mirror of Scripture, the Constitution, and the Declaration of Independence to call America to account for the racism that was a glaring contradiction to our foundational principles. Both creation and the person and work of Christ militate against ethnic partiality—the first because we are all descendants of the same people, and the other because:

> For through him we both have access in one Spirit to the Father. So then you are no longer strangers and aliens, but you are fellow citizens with the saints and members of the household of God, built on the foundation of the apostles and prophets, Christ Jesus himself being the cornerstone, in whom the whole structure, being joined together, grows into a holy temple in the Lord. In him you also are being built together into a dwelling place for God by the Spirit. (Ephesians 2:18–22)

While this passage makes it clear that there is no room for racism, and that the *Loving* decision violates fundamental biblical truth, the same cannot be said of same-sex marriage. There is no basis upon which to argue that the definition of marriage has ever, or should ever, include people of the same sex. On the contrary, thousands of years of history and sacred texts prove the opposite. Unfortunately, that history and those sacred texts have been supplanted by another standard.

This new standard originates from the work of a few key twentieth-century thinkers whose work laid the foundation for the ideologies that rule our times. We'll discuss those in detail in the next chapter.

CHAPTER 3

The Founders of the Feast

There are a few key figures whose work undergirds most of the modern "woke" movement and its panoply of sexual expressions. They all relied heavily on lies, as well as a host of other abjectly horrifying things, to produce it—and they did so knowingly. I'll explain to you what happened in chronological order so you can see how this foundation was built, step by methodical step, to help you understand how we arrived at the current state of our culture, and where we're headed.

A discussion of the key figures and ideas that led to our current ideological moment could fill volumes.[1] We could talk about Sigmund Freud's contribution to the sexualization of the field of psychology, or Michel Foucault's radical views on power dynamics and how they transformed the way we view language. Then there is the influential work of queer theorists like Judith Butler and the revolutionary ideas of Frankfurt School thinkers Adorno, Horkheimer, and Marcuse. However, for our purposes, there are four men whose work has contributed more to contemporary thinking and attitudes on sexuality and sexual identity than just about any others. You may not know their names, but I guarantee you have been impacted by their work.

Alfred Kinsey

If you have any interest in the issue of modern sexuality, you've undoubtedly heard of Alfred Kinsey—but you probably don't know that he was a sadomasochist, a voyeur, and a child abuser. But all of this is evident to anyone willing to look closely at his work.

In 1948, Kinsey published a book that is considered the gold standard for understanding human sexuality, *Sexual Behavior in the Human Male*. What most people don't know is that one of Kinsey's primary research methods was watching pedophiles molest young children. In one of his more mind-boggling revelations, he wrote,

> Some of these adults are technically trained persons who have kept diaries or other records which have been put at our disposal; and from them we have secured information on 317 preadolescents who were either observed in self masturbation, *or who were observed in contacts with other boys or older adults*.[2] (emphasis mine)

Elsewhere, Kinsey notes that his records were based on what he identified as

> more or less uninhibited boys, most of whom had heard about sex and seen sexual activities among their companions, and many of whom had had sexual contacts with one or more adults.[3]

But is this not the most revolting aspect of Kinsey's "research." I am loathe to include his material on "infant orgasm," but I think it is necessary to do so here for two main reasons. First, it is important to expose such darkness. I am guided here by Paul's words in Ephesians 5:

> But sexual immorality and all impurity or covetousness must not even be named among you, as is proper among saints. Let there be no filthiness nor foolish talk nor crude joking, which are out of place, but instead let there be thanksgiving. For you may be sure of this, that everyone who is sexually immoral or impure, or who is covetous (that is, an idolater), has no inheritance in the kingdom of Christ and God. Let no one deceive you with empty words, for because of these things the wrath of God comes upon the sons of disobedience. Therefore do not become partners with them; for at one time you were darkness, but now you are light in the Lord. Walk as children of light (for the fruit of light is found in all that is good and right and true), and try to discern what is pleasing to the Lord. *Take no part in the unfruitful works of darkness, but instead expose them.* For it is shameful even to speak of the things that they do in secret. (Ephesians 5:3–12, emphasis mine)

The second reason I am persuaded to expose these despicable truths is because, if we find this material offensive, why do we so unquestioningly accept it as the basis for our understanding of human sexuality? Even if you don't personally accept it as such, you'd better believe your local school board, university, medical professionals, and politicians do. Kinsey is viewed as a modern-day hero. Harry Hay, one of Kinsey's interviewees and one of the earliest and most prominent gay activists "carried the *Kinsey Report* with him everywhere, like a religious zealot carrying around a Bible."[4] But who was the author of this "Bible"?

Kinsey the Voyeuristic Pedophile

Before the fiftieth anniversary of Kinsey's book in 1997, the leftist publication Salon sang its praises:

> The history of sex in America falls into two large, unequal, yet clearly defined periods. The first era belonged to the Puritans, the Victorians. . . . This epoch of libidinal prohibition lasted until Jan. 4, 1948. The following day, Professor Alfred C. Kinsey of Indiana published *Sexual Behavior in the Human Male*. Whereupon, as the expression has it, the earth moved.[5]

But in which direction did the earth move? The late author Judith Reisman was among those who believed it moved backward and downward. Prolific Catholic author E. Michael Jones described a seminal moment when Reisman publicly called out Kinsey's fraudulent and debased work in front of a crowd filled with his academic progeny in 1981 when she

> delivered a paper [titled] "The Scientist as a Contributing Agent to Child Sexual Abuse: A Preliminary Study," in which she brought up for the first time in the thirty-two years since it had been published the material on child sexuality in Tables 30–34 of the Kinsey *Male* volume

and wondered how this data could have been obtained without involvement in criminal activity. Before giving her report, Reisman had written to *Male* volume coauthor Paul Gebhard to ask about the data in Tables 30–34. Gebhard wrote back saying that the data had been obtained from parents, schoolteachers, and some male homosexuals, including "some of Kinsey's men" who had used "manual and oral techniques" to catalogue the number of orgasms they said they could stimulate in infants and children. Virtually the entire sex industry–sex research establishment worldwide was in attendance at the meeting in Jerusalem, but the reaction to the talk was silence, stunned or sullen or otherwise, until a Swedish reporter wondered out loud why the assembled experts had nothing to say.[6]

But why the stunned silence? Jones explains that it was "understandable":

> Just about everyone in attendance had cited Kinsey as their mentor, and some even knew about the criminal activity involved in Kinsey's research. They all knew that Kinsey's research was the basis of their "science," which is to say, the legitimizing basis for everything they did. Kinsey was the foundation of that house of cards. If what he had done could be discredited, it threatened the sexual empire which had been built since his death and upon which they all depended for a livelihood. Later when word got out that Reisman had government money to pursue her thesis and show a link between Kinsey' s exploitation

of child "sexuality" and *Playboy*, *Penthouse*, and *Hustler*'s exploitation of the same thing, stunned silence turned to determined, if behind the scenes, action.[7]

What was so scandalous about Tables 30–34? Those are the tables cataloguing Kinsey's research on "preadolescent orgasm." In them, he notes that

> Orgasm has been observed in boys of every age from five months to adolescence (Table 31). Orgasm is in our records for a female babe of four months. . . . The orgasm in an infant or other young male is, except for the lack of an ejaculation, a striking duplicate of orgasm in an older adult.[8]

Then, in an entry that should have landed him in jail, he writes,

> A fretful babe quiets down under the initial sexual stimulation, is distracted from other activities, begins rhythmic pelvic thrusts, becomes tense as climax approaches, is thrown into convulsive action, often with violent arm and leg movements, sometimes with weeping at the moment of climax.[9]

The only thing more sickening than this is the lasting impact those studies have had. As a writer for the *Epoch Times* noted in 2020, "Very few people realize that the reason children today are being sexualized at school is because pedophiles sexually abused hundreds of children, then claimed that the victims enjoyed it."[10]

Reisman told us, "Kinsey solicited and encouraged pedophiles, at home and abroad, to sexually violate from 317 to

2,035 infants and children for his alleged data on normal 'child sexuality.'"[11]

Kinsey the Sadomasochist

Kinsey was a sadist in every sense of the word. By late adolescence, his masochism was well advanced, inserting various objects into his urethra.[12] Later, he participated in bondage, domination, and sadomasochism,[13] but that was not the height of his disordered behavior. Kinsey turned "masturbation itself into an act of penance; tough enough to punish himself with savage brutality."[14] I write this not to be crude, but to point out the obvious connection between Kinsey's pathological fascination with sadomasochistic masturbation and his sex research (much of which involved encouraging children to masturbate).

Kinsey the Voyeur

Kinsey was not only a sadomasochist, he also had a penchant for voyeurism. Perhaps this explains what motivated him to conduct the kind of research he did.

It started when he was a boy, "sneaking glimpses of [other] boys while they dressed, watching them in the shower."[15] Later, it grew into a fetish that, in 1949, led him to "put aside a budget of $10,000 for photographic equipment"[16] that he used to film himself, his colleagues, and their wives engaging in various sex acts. How did he get them to agree to that?

According to [his photographer], Kinsey had a gift for making outrageous requests appear reasonable. Kinsey accomplished this by arguing that because the [Kinsey] Institute was investigating sex there should be no shame or guilt or repugnance attached to any sexual activity among senior staff members. In other words, he assumed his familiar role as teacher, the mentor who knew how to show less liberated souls the path to sexual freedom.[17]

In later years, one of Kinsey's colleagues' wives complained of "the sickening pressure" she was under to have sex on film with her spouse and other staff members at Kinsey's "research" firm. She told an interviewer, "I felt like my husband's career at the Institute depended on it."[18]

Try to imagine a scientist/researcher in any field today who was known to have forced a woman to film sex acts in order to protect her husband's job. Not even Harvey Weinstein stooped so low. Yet that is the legacy of Alfred Kinsey, the father of modern sexology! And that's not even what negates the value of his scientific contribution.

Kinsey the Fraudulent Researcher

On top of Kinsey's sadomasochism and voyeurism, his research was completely fraudulent. Reisman offered the following summary:

> Kinsey's closet team 1) "forced" subjects to give the desired answers to their sex questions, 2) secretly trashed three-quarters of their research data, and 3) based their claims about normal males on a roughly 86 percent aberrant male population including 200 sexual psychopaths, 1,400 sex offenders, and hundreds each of prisoners, male prostitutes, and promiscuous homosexuals.[19]

Kinsey's work was used to validate the idea that children are sexual from birth and that what we consider to be "deviant" behavior really isn't. As we watch the world at large embrace the normalization of multiple kinds of sexual perversions, pedophilia gain greater acceptance, and government schools become bastions for the grooming and molestation of children, remember this: The fraudulent work of Alfred Kinsey, the sadomasochistic, voyeuristic pedophile, is the playbook the people pushing those things are all using.

John Money

A few years after the publication of Kinsey's book, John Money embarked on a scientific journey that would lead the field of sexology even further down the rabbit hole.

Bruce Reimer and his twin brother, Brian, were born in Winnipeg, Canada, on August 22, 1965.[20] A few months later, their mother noticed the boys were having problems urinating. After discussing the issue, the Reimers decided to have the boys circumcised—and that's when Bruce's life changed forever: His surgery came first, and the doctor botched the circumcision. That irreparable injury led his parents to take him to see a famed sex researcher at the prestigious Johns Hopkins Hospital in Baltimore: Dr. John Money.

Money convinced the Reimers to allow him to perform gender-reassignment surgery on Bruce, and then submit both him and Brian to an ongoing research study. The couple had no idea what they had just agreed to permit their sons to endure. Because Bruce was a twin, Brian "provided to the experiment a built-in matched control—a genetic clone who, with penis and testicles intact, was raised as a male."[21] Like his acolytes throughout academia, medicine, and government today, Money believed gender is socially constructed, and therefore believed Bruce could be raised as "Brenda" and function as a normal "woman" at the end of his treatment.

Money was fascinated by hermaphrodism—a rare medical disorder in which a baby is born with both male and female reproductive organs. And he dedicated his life to proving to the world that psychologically, we are all hermaphrodites.[22]

Therefore, Bruce was renamed "Brenda" and raised as a female.

The process involved clinical castration and other genital surgery . . . followed by a twelve-year program of social, mental, and hormonal conditioning to make the transformation take hold in his psyche.[23]

The case was reported in the medical literature as an unqualified success, and Bruce/Brenda became one of the most famous (though unnamed) patients in the annals of modern medicine.[24]

Money has recounted how he spelled out to the [Reimers] the advantages of sex reassignment for their baby—"using non-technical words, diagrams, and photographs of children who had been reassigned." He explained . . . that their baby could be given a perfectly functional vagina—"adequate for sexual intercourse and for sexual pleasure, including orgasm." He also explained to them that although their child would not, if changed into a girl, be able to bear children, she would develop psychologically as a woman and would find her erotic attraction to men.

As a married woman she would be perfectly capable of adopting children of her own.[25]

The impact was massive! "Textbooks in medicine and the social sciences were rewritten to include the case, and a precedent for infant sex reassignment as standard treatment in cases of newborns with injured or irregular genitals was established."[26]

Not only are Money's arguments still being used in the burgeoning field of sex reassignment today, but they are now being expanded upon by counselors who claim that giving puberty-blocking drugs to young children and adolescents is harmless and the effects reversible (a lie).[27] But the medical field was not the only one paying attention to Money's work: The case was crucial for the feminist movement in the 1970s and was often cited by those who argued the gender gap was purely a result of cultural conditioning, not biology.[28]

But hermaphrodism was not Money's sole interest.

Money the Pedophile

[L]ike the good Dr. Kinsey, John Money believed sex between adults and children could be beneficial. He was a proponent of adult–child love, even incest. . . . Money crusaded against traditional morality, arguing that ancient taboos were destructive.[29]

One of his theories of how children form their different gender schemas was that they must understand at an early age the differences between male and female sex organs.

During their yearly visits, Money firmly, loudly, and angrily told the [Reimer boys] to take off their clothes, look at each other's genitalia, and act out sexual intercourse.[30]

According to Money, pornography was ideal for this purpose. "[E]xplicit sexual pictures," he wrote in his book *Sexual Signatures*, "can and should be used as part of a child's sex education." Such pictures, he said, "reinforce [the child's] own gender identity/role."[31]

There was just one problem. The whole thing was a lie!

In his book *As Nature Made Him*, John Colapinto exposes Money's lies in telling the Reimers' heartbreaking story. At the age of fourteen, Bruce grew tired of struggling with his imposed girlhood and "reverted to the sex written in his genes and chromosomes."[32] He also changed his name to "David" in an effort to put the whole sordid episode behind him.

In 2004, at age thirty-eight, Bruce/Brenda/David Reimer committed suicide. Tragically, Brian, who was also abused in Money's experiments, later died of a drug overdose.

Dr. Miriam Grossman—an author and board-certified child and adolescent psychologist who is one of the seeming few still standing for the truths of biology and science—notes that "the entire gender ideology, and all these clinics and hospitals and gender education and the flags and the whole movement—which has become a civil rights moment basically—is entirely based on a concept that was never proven."[33]

So why, given the fact that both Kinsey's and Money's research has been disproven, do we still live in a world where their fraudulent ideas are treated as gospel? To answer that question, we have to turn our attention from two important researchers to two important marketing experts.

The Most Important Book You've Never Read

Marshall Kirk and Hunter Madsen were Harvard University professors who taught marketing and psychology, respectively, in the 1980s. They teamed up in 1989 to write a book called *After the Ball: How America Will Overcome Its Fear and Hatred of Gays in the 90s*. AIDS was rampant at the time, and people were blaming the gay community for it. Lillian Faderman captures their perspective on that period in her critically acclaimed book, *The Gay Revolution: The Story of the Struggle*:

> The Far Right did not waste the shock value. Paleo-conservative Patrick Buchanan gloated in his syndicated column that AIDS was a sign that "Nature is exacting retribution"; but now, he wrote, not only were these homosexuals a "moral menace," they were a "public health menace," too. Buchanan reported that policemen were so worried about getting AIDS and bringing it home to their families that they had to don masks and gloves when dealing with homosexual lawbreakers; landlords were so worried about the spread of AIDS on their premises that they had to evict infected homosexuals from their property. Because of homosexuals' morally irresponsible and unhealthy sex practices, they were the spreaders of a host of other diseases, too, that could affect innocent heterosexuals, such as hepatitis. Therefore, Buchanan ranted, they must not be allowed to work in restaurants or any job in which they handled food. "Gay rights"—homosexuals' demands to live and work wherever they wanted—were dangerous to heterosexuals.[34]

In the midst of all the furor over AIDS, Kirk and Madsen hatched a plan to turn the tables:

> AIDS, though a loose cannon, is a cannon indeed. As cynical as it may seem, AIDS gives us a chance, however brief, to establish ourselves as a victimized minority legitimately deserving of America's special protection and care. This, therefore, is the question and the challenge: how can we surmount our "insurmountable" opportunity? How can we maximize the sympathy and minimize the fear? How, given the horrid hand that AIDS has dealt us, can we best play it?[35]

Before we look at their specific strategies, you should know that their understanding of human sexuality is based on Kinsey's research which gives rise to the assumptions underlying their arguments in *After the Ball*. For instance, they argue that "Alfred Kinsey and his colleagues . . . gathered *nationally representative data* . . . on the incidence of homosexual experience among American men and women."[36] They go on to assert that "the Kinsey surveys provide the most reliable data yet available on this sensitive topic."[37] In fact, their repeated reference to the statistic that "one in ten" Americans is gay is derived from Kinsey's research. They state, "If we must draw the line somewhere and pick a specific percentage for propaganda purposes, we may as well stick with the solidly conservative figure suggested by Kinsey decades ago."[38]

The Strategy
The campaign, they wrote, "though complex, depends centrally upon a program of unabashed propaganda, firmly grounded in

long-established principles of psychology and advertising."[39] If you find it surprising that they used the word "propaganda," you will find it even more surprising in light of the fact that they went on to define it as communication that:

1. Relies on emotional manipulation,
2. Uses lies, and
3. Is subjective and one-sided.

> [I]t makes no difference that the ads are lies; not to us, because we're using them to ethically good effect . . . [to t]ell our side of the story as movingly as possible. In the battle for hearts and minds, effective propaganda knows enough to put its best foot forward . . . this is what our own media campaign must do.[40]

This propaganda campaign had three main parts: desensitizing, jamming, and conversion. Kirk and Madsen were also honest enough to admit that these are the three steps used in brainwashing. The methodology goes as follows:

Desensitizing

"To desensitize straights to gays and gayness," Kirk and Madsen believed they must first

> inundate them in a continuous flood of gay-related advertising, presented in the least offensive fashion possible. . . . If straights can't shut off the shower, they may at least eventually get used to being wet.[41]

In the early stages of the campaign, the public should not be shocked and repelled by premature exposure to homosexual behavior itself. Instead, the imagery of sex *per se* should be downplayed, and the issue of gay rights reduced, as far as possible, to an abstract social question.[42]

Hence, while today we are constantly bombarded with same-sex relationships and sexual encounters on television, in movies, and even commercials, earlier media portrayals did not involve sexual relationships. Instead, gay characters were the wisest, wittiest ones who served as the moral compass of the show (i.e., Will of *Will & Grace*).

Another place where desensitization is in full swing is the news media. As far back as the late 1990s or early 2000s, Reisman tells us, "The National Lesbian and Gay Journalists Association (NLGJA) . . . boasted that although homosexuals make up less than 2 percent of the population, three-fourths of the people who decide the content of the front page of the *New York Times* are homosexual."[43]

Children's programming is the new frontier of the desensitizing agenda. According to Insider.com, as of 2020 there were 259 confirmed gay characters in children's television programs.[44]

The way baby boomers once learned to rattle off state capitals, elementary school kids are now taught today's gender taxonomy often enough to commit it to memory.[45]

The year-long Pride Parade often begins in October with "Coming Out Day," "International Pronouns Day," and LGBTQ History Month; November brings "Transgender Awareness Week," capped off by "Transgender Day of

Remembrance," a vigil for transgender individuals killed for this identity. March is "Transgender Visibility Month." April contributes "Day of Silence / Day of Action" to spread awareness of bullying and harassment of LGBTQ students. May offers "Harvey Milk Day," dedicated to mourning the prominent gay rights activist; and June, of course, is Pride Month—thirty days dedicated to celebrating LGBTQ identities and decrying anti-LGBTQ oppression.[46]

As this book was being written, a school district in Southern California bowed to state pressure in order to avoid a lawsuit. The issue? Local school board members in Temecula, led by a conservative majority, had elected not to use a new curriculum forcing students to learn about Harvey Milk. As a result, Governor Gavin Newsom threatened to fine the district $1.5 million for defying state law, and even send the new state-approved textbooks directly to students if need be.[47]

That's how much progress desensitization has made since 1989.

Jamming

The second phase of Kirk and Madsen's propaganda strategy was the jamming phase, during which it would be particularly important to "accuse religious people" of bigotry and hypocrisy. To do so, they reasoned that "[g]ays can use talk . . . to undercut the rationalizations that 'justify' religious bigotry and to jam some of its psychic rewards." Specifically, this could be done if homosexuals "portray [anti-gay] institutions as antiquated backwaters, badly out of step with the times and with the latest findings of psychology."[48] In a particularly telling passage, they suggest:

> propagandist advertisement can depict homophobic and homohating bigots as crude loudmouths and assholes—people who say not only "faggot" but "nigger," "kike," and other shameful epithets—who are "not Christian." It can show them being criticized, hated, shunned. It can depict gays experiencing horrific suffering as the direct result of the homohatred—suffering of which even most bigots would be ashamed to be the cause. It can, in short, link homohating bigotry with all sorts of attributes the bigot would be ashamed to possess, and with social consequences he would find unpleasant and scary.[49]

The other side of this coin is the suppression of other relevant facts. For example, we hear frequently about hate crimes against homosexuals. However, we don't hear that a large number of those alleged hate crimes are actually hoaxes, or that rates of violence between homosexual partners far outpaces violence from those outside the relationship.[50, 51] For example, in their book *Men Who Beat the Men Who Love Them,* David Island and Patrick Letellier note, "It is . . . likely . . . that the incidence of domestic violence among gay men is nearly double that in the heterosexual population."[52]

Conversion

While desensitization and jamming are crucial to the *After the Ball* strategy, they are merely means to an end: conversion.[53]

Contrary to the way it sounds, conversion is not about turning straight people gay. Rather, it is ideological work. "It isn't enough that antigay bigots should become confused about us, or even indifferent to us," admit Kirk and Madsen; "we are safest, in the long run, if we can actually make them like us."[54]

But conversion is about a lot more than merely "liking" gay people or other "sexual minorities": It is about changing worldviews. Kirk and Madsen wanted nothing less than "conversion of the average American's emotions, mind, and will through a planned psychological attack, in the form of propaganda fed to the nation via the media [and the schools]."[55]

This is the process that has led elementary schoolchildren to question their gender or insist they are cats and turned baby boomers into allies. Conversion is the process that led dozens of Republicans to help pass the so-called federal "Respect for Marriage Act" in December 2022 and has led to compromise in several evangelical denominations. In short, conversion is the process that has changed the moral and political landscape of our nation within a single generation.

From Conversion to Coercion

In 1987, Steve Warren wrote one of the most honest, alarming, and prescient cautions ever delivered by an LGBTQ activist. "Warning to Homophobes," published in the leading gay publication *The Advocate* in 1987, came across like the ravings of a madman; today, it comes across as prophetic.

1. Henceforth, homosexuality will be spoken of in your churches and synagogues as an "honorable estate."

2. You can either let us marry people of the same sex, or better yet abolish marriage altogether. . . .

3. You will be expected to offer ceremonies that bless our sexual arrangements. . . . You will also instruct your people in homosexual as well as heterosexual behavior, and you will go out of your way to make certain that homosexual youths are allowed to date, attend religious functions together, openly display affection, and enjoy each other's sexuality without embarrassment or guilt.

4. If any of the older people in your midst object, you will deal with them sternly, making certain they renounce their ugly and ignorant homophobia or suffer public humiliation.

5. You will also make certain that . . . laws are passed forbidding discrimination against homosexuals and heavy punishments are assessed. . . .

6. Finally, we will in all likelihood want to expunge a number of passages from your Scriptures and rewrite others, eliminating preferential treatment of marriage and using words that will allow for homosexual interpretations of passages describing biblical lovers such as Ruth and Boaz or Solomon and the Queen of Sheba.

    Warning: If all these things do not come to pass quickly, we will subject Orthodox Jews and Christians to the most sustained hatred and vilification in recent memory. We have captured the liberal establishment and the press. We have already beaten you on a number of battlefields. . . . You have neither the faith nor the strength to fight us, so you might as well surrender now.[56]

What Lies Ahead

One of the inevitable consequences of the "gay is the new black" paradigm is the eventual elimination of religious freedom protections. Several Republicans justified their support of the "Respect for Marriage Act"—which protects same-sex marriages nationwide from federal nullification even if the U.S. Supreme Court someday overturns *Obergefell*—by denying this inevitable reality. However, this rationale is naïve at best. If it is true that homosexuality is as innate and immutable as race and forbidding same-sex marriage is tantamount to antimiscegenation, then it must follow that allowing the church to discriminate against same-sex marriage (or other types of marriage that have yet to gain that kind of mainstream acceptance) is as morally reprehensible as *Loving v. Virginia*. At the time of this writing, the coercion is limited to moral pressure applied by institutions—but the day will come, and probably not long from now, when the full weight of the law will be brought to bear on churches that hold to a biblical view of marriage and ensure that their orthopraxy matches their orthodoxy.

There is a long list of "sexual minorities" who are now poised to capitalize upon the gay community's successes in hijacking the rationale that led to black Americans' victories in the civil rights movement. We'll take a closer look at those groups in the next chapter.

CHAPTER 4

The Ubiquitous, Ever-Growing, Self-Contradictory Acronym—Part I

LGBT

The growing and malleable acronym, LGBTQIA2S+, is as inconsistent as it is ubiquitous. Consequently, it remains a mystery to many. In this chapter, I will not only explain what the letters of the acronym mean, I will also show why many of them are inherently contradictory to the point of negating one another.

The Flag

During Pride Month festivities at the White House in 2023, I noticed, among other things, that there was a new flag hanging from the balcony of the West Wing. This flag incorporated the familiar rainbow flag, but also had additional designs. I wasn't sure what to make of it, so I looked it up. In doing so, I got quite the education on not only the rainbow flag, but the political and ideological transformation it has undergone.

For instance, the original flag, created by Gilbert Baker in 1978, was comprised of eight colored stripes stacked on top of each other, not the six we see today. I also learned that Baker assigned a specific meaning to each color: pink for sex, red for life, orange for healing, yellow for sunlight, green for nature, turquoise for magic, indigo for serenity, and violet for spirit. In 1979, the pink was dropped due to a shortage of pink fabric, and indigo and turquoise were replaced with blue due to concerns about the legibility of the lighter colors.

The flag hanging from the White House in 2023 was the Progress Pride flag, developed in 2018 by nonbinary American artist and designer Daniel Quasar.[1] It is a combination of several ideological flags, including the transgender flag, created by Monica Helms in 1999; the Philadelphia City Hall pride flag, which added black and brown stripes in 2017 to highlight the discrimination against black and brown people, and the Seattle pride flag, which added five new colors to the 1979 rainbow flag in 2018.

The L and the G (It's All in the Biology . . . Right?)

The acronym is based on the L (lesbian) and the G (gay). These two are foundational both in terms of their longevity, presence, and political power. The gay and lesbian movement started fighting for civil rights long before the other acronyms joined the fray.[2]

As early as the 1950s, groups like the Mattachine Society, founded by early gay-rights and Communist activist Harry Hay (who also was an active supporter of the North American Man-Boy Love Association), were pushing for the "rights" of what in the beginning were almost exclusively gay men. Later, groups like the Daughters of Bilitis would highlight the plight of lesbians. Eventually, the two would come together to form other organizations that conflated the lesbian and gay agendas to form the homosexual movement.[3]

Today, it is almost universally assumed that homosexuality is a matter of orientation rather than preference or proclivity, despite the fact that there is no conclusive evidence supporting the idea. Of course, the term "orientation" is almost always defined either loosely or not at all by those who use it. We know there are no biological markers that can predict homosexuality, despite numerous attempts to prove a biological cause. Even propagandists like Kirk and Madsen, who "argue that . . . gays should be considered to have been born gay," admit that "sexual orientation . . . seems to be the product of a complex interaction between innate predispositions and environmental factors during childhood and early adolescence."[4] And subsequent studies have failed to prove otherwise:

During the last forty years the majority of [same-sex attraction] studies have been conducted, reviewed and/or published by homosexuality-affirming researchers, many of whom are also openly homosexual. Virtually all of the studies were touted by the media as proving that SSA is inborn. In reality, however, every one of them, from gene analysis to brain structure, fingerprint styles, handedness, finger lengths, eye blinking, ear characteristics, verbal skills and prenatal hormones, have failed to be replicated, were criticized for research limitations, and/or were out-right debunked.[5]

Nor would this make a difference. A biological cause for homo-sexuality would do no more to change the sinfulness of the behavior than would a biological cause for anger, addiction, or pedophilia. (Interestingly enough, pedophiles are currently mak-ing the same argument for their "orientation" as lesbians and gay men.[6] But they are not a part of the acronym . . . yet.)

Another factor showing that homosexuality is not innate is the fact that it can be "triggered." In her 2009 book *Sexual Fluidity: Understanding Women's Love and Desire*, Lisa Diamond exam-ined research showing that

> One facilitating factor may be heightened physical close-ness and contact. Some girls and women have the poten-tial of being profoundly influenced, in both thought and behavior, by their environment: a class on feminism, joining a political organization, attending an all-girls school. (In fact, students at Smith College joke that the college motto should be "Queer in a year or your money back.") And, for girls, awareness of same-sex attraction often follows questioning instead of preceding it. That is, girls don't question because they feel attracted to their friend; they feel attracted to their friend as a result of questioning.[7]

As an addendum to the point about Smith College above, research has indicated that a college education increases wom-en's likelihood of identifying as lesbian by a factor of nine.[8]

Miriam Grossman is a practicing psychiatrist who is concerned about current trends in gender ideology. She disagrees with the assertion that sexual orientation is immutable. In her book *You're Teaching My Kids What?*, she recalls a time when she had to confront the fact that people's sexual orientation is changeable. After attending a group therapy session with several ex-gays, she

> had an idea: Invite these remarkable men to come and speak to my colleagues at the counseling center. Have them describe their journeys to therapists who are convinced that therapy for unwanted same-sex attraction is wrong and dangerous. Here's a chance for open discussion of an urgent topic.[9]

The men were all for it. "Just tell us when and where—we'll be there," they promised. "Sounds fascinating," her director responded. However, the university wouldn't go for it. To say that Grossman was disappointed would be an understatement. "Well, so much for being open-minded," she thought. "So much for celebrating intellectual debate, diversity, tolerance, and multiculturalism. And so much for a patient's right to self-determination."[10]

Grossman believes educators and therapists, with their intolerance of diverse views, harm students like the ones she observed by neglecting to inform them that alternatives to gay-affirming therapy exist, thereby depriving them of the right to self-determination. Without choices, they are left to struggle with their unwanted same-sex impulses alone—leaving them without hope, and thereby worsening their emotional distress.

By and large, Grossman's colleagues in psychiatry believe "that efforts to change sexual orientation are futile" and therefore don't want to consider them at all.[11] But if honest researchers had the opportunity to speak with men like the ones she's met, she says, they wouldn't be so quick to declare, "Therapy cannot change one's sexual orientation."[12]

The B (It's Biology . . . But)

Bisexuals, according to *Merriam-Webster's Dictionary*, are "characterized by sexual or romantic attraction to people of one's same sex and of the opposite sex."[13] Note the lack of any biological indication in that definition. This is simply a matter of "sexual or romantic attraction." However, the ever-growing acronym insists that we are talking about people as they are and ever shall be. In other words, it's just like being black.

Shiri Eisner is a bisexual activist and the author of *Bi: Notes for a Revolution*. She suggests asking yourself the following questions to determine if you're bisexual:

- Does the term "bisexual" give me a sense of comfort?
- Does the term "bisexual" give me a sense of adventure?
- Is it fun for me to think about being bisexual?
- Does the thought of being bisexual or identifying as bisexual make me happy?
- Does it make me feel good about myself?
- Does the term "bisexuality" give me a sense of challenge?
- Does it give me community? Or support?
- Does it give me anything else I want?[14]

Remember, the argument is that bisexuality is an "orientation" like being lesbian or gay. These are supposedly as innate
and immutable as ethnicity, yet questions like, "Does the term
bisexual give me a sense of comfort?" are supposedly relevant to discovering whether one has this innate, immutable
orientation.

According to a 2021 Gallup poll, 57 percent of all Americans
who identify as LGBT indicate they are bisexual.[15] Of course,
this too is changing rapidly. As genderqueer ideology takes hold,
I predict increasingly fewer people will limit themselves to the
passé, uninteresting bisexual designation. In fact, we are already
seeing a sharp, generational increase in the number of people
who identify as LGBT, with the most rapid growth coming in
the T category (see chart).[16] According to a guaranteed income
program in San Francisco, there are more than 100 sexuality
options to choose from.[17]

	LGBT	Straight/Heterosexual
	%	%
Generation Z (born 1997–2003)	20.8	75.7
Millennials (born 1981–1996)	10.5	82.5
Generation X (born 1965–1980)	4.2	89.3
Baby Boomers (born 1946–1964)	2.6	90.7
Traditionalists (born before 1946)	0.8	92.2 Source: Gallup

The T (Biology Is Irrelevant)

Unless you live under a rock, you are well aware that we are in the midst of a transgender revolution. The conventional "wisdom" is that gender and sex are unrelated concepts. Sex has to do with our biology; gender is about our roles. Sex is "assigned" at birth. Gender is learned and shaped by culture. At least that's what we're told. All of this is false.

"Until at least two and a half years of age," notes Dr. Miriam Grossman, "children are unable to consistently label themselves—or discriminate between—male and female." This is important because, "That's a year or more after showing a preference for the doll or the truck"—preferences, we are told, that are imposed on children. Grossman's conclusion is obvious: "How can children choose particular toys based on what's expected of them as a girl or boy, before grasping the concept of girl or boy?"[18] Yet, the conventional wisdom prevails. We continue to believe the lie being perpetuated in popular culture.

In 2015, Olympic gold medalist Bruce Jenner changed his name to Caitlyn and took home the Arthur Ashe Courage Award at the ESPYS,[19] then was named one of *Glamour Magazine*'s Women of the Year a few months later.[20] Will Thomas swam unremarkably for three years on the University of Pennsylvania's men's team before sitting out a year while undergoing testosterone suppression treatment and changing his name to Lia; upon his return, he competed—and dominated his competition—as a woman, taking home the NCAA 500-meter championship medal. The University of Pennsylvania added insult to injury by nominating Thomas for the 2022 NCAA Woman of the Year award.[21] At press time, Thomas was also considering a run at the 2024 women's Olympic swim team.

If that happens, Thomas would not be the first male-to-female transgender athlete to compete in the Olympics: In 2021, New Zealand's Laurel Hubbard competed in weightlifting at the Tokyo Games. Chelsea Wolfe, a transgender cyclist, was a reserve on the U.S. women's BMX freestyle team. And who can forget Quinn (that's it . . . just Quinn, no last name), who became the first openly transgender athlete to participate in the Olympics when "they" started in Canada's opening soccer match against Japan.

Such things are also taking place in government. In 2021, Rachel Levine was confirmed as the assistant secretary of the U.S. Department of Health and Human Services.[22] Let that sink in: A man who identifies as a woman is one of the highest-ranking health officials in the United States. No wonder Judge Ketanji Brown Jackson dodged when Senator Marsha Blackburn asked her, "What is a woman?" during her confirmation hearings for the U.S. Supreme Court. The exchange was one for the ages:

> **Blackburn:** Can you provide a definition for the word woman?
> **Jackson:** Can I provide a definition? No, I can't.
> **Blackburn:** You can't?
> **Jackson:** Not in this context. I'm not a biologist.[23]

Ironically, Jackson's answer runs afoul of trans ideology since, according to trans doctrine, biology is irrelevant.

As with the triggering of lesbianism, there is currently an epidemic of trans identification among teen girls. Abigail Shrier's controversial book, *Irreversible Damage*, offers unsettling insight into the phenomenon.

By the end of seventh grade, Faith's daughter decided she was "asexual," and then "trans." She had never even kissed a boy, had not yet gotten her period. But the new identity gave her both a cause and a team.[24]

This sense of belonging is a major aspect of the recent uptick among young girls.

"All her friends are bisexual," her mother told me, a year after her daughter's announcement. "There's only one heterosexual girl in her little crew. Everybody else is lesbian, bisexual. My daughter had to one-up them and be 'trans.'"[25]

If you cannot fathom this situation, it may be because you are disconnected from many of its root causes and influences:

You grew up differently. You didn't suffer the acute isolation of today's teenagers. You didn't soak your retinas in the internet's transgender propaganda during a confusing time in your life. And you didn't attend today's public schools, many of which provide K–12 indoctrination in gender ideology that is both so radical and so pervasive that it is hardly surprising so many kids might want to take cover under an LGBTQ umbrella.[26]

Shrier notes that the schools are not forcing adolescents to identify as trans,

but they are greasing the skids. The LGBTQ safe house they've fashioned is avant garde and enticing, framed with moral superiority, insulated with civil rights. Those who teach gender ideology do not make adolescents transgender. They simply fill kids' heads with gender options and ideology. Then, when the adolescents do experience a crisis, the heroic solution readily bobs to mind.[27]

All of these things hearken back to John Money's research. And the movement is gaining steam.

Gender-Affirming "Care"

In light of Money's experiments, one would think the medical industry would change course on its treatment and analysis of gender dysphoria. One would be wrong. The entire apparatus continues to march forward as though Money's work was the shining success it was fraudulently claimed to have been. Sex education is not about health—it's a social movement, a vehicle for changing the world. It happens one child at a time, and it goes on right under your nose.[28]

California boasts the most comprehensive statewide gender identity and sexual orientation instruction, statutorily mandatory for all students enrolled in grades K–12 and explicitly barring parental opt-out. A clever legerdemain enabled this feat. California law explicitly allows parental opt-out from sexual health education. But the California legislature exempted all materials related to "gender identity, gender expression" and "sexual orientation" from that opt-out. Such instruction—educators contend—is essential to prevent discrimination, harassment, and bullying. In order to protect gay and trans kids from harassment, in other words, it was necessary for all children to receive gender identity and sexual orientation instruction.[29]

Girls who like math, sports, or are logical, and boys who sing, act, or like to draw are all "gender nonconforming." They may have gone to school as a "girl who excels at math" or "boy with vocal talent," but they leave rebranded as "a person whose behaviors or gender expression falls outside what is generally considered typical for their assigned sex at birth."[30]

This is how gender ideology is taught in schools: with the materials, curricula, speakers, and teacher training supplied by gender activists. Kindergarteners are introduced to the "Genderbread Person" and "Gender Unicorn." Kindergarten teachers read from *I Am Jazz*, and the little ones are taught that they might have a "girl brain in a boy body" or vice versa.[31]

Society used to believe that the Y chromosome was only associated with growing a beard, male genitalia, etc. Now we know the Y chromosome affects every organ system in the human body. In fact, there is an entire field of medicine dealing with this reality.

> The field of gender-specific medicine examines how normal human biology and physiology differ between men and women and how the diagnosis and treatment of disease differs as a function of gender and sex. Among the areas of greatest difference are cardiovascular disease, mood disorders, the immune system, cancer, osteoporosis, diabetes, obesity, and infectious diseases.[32]

How does this jibe with the idea that sex is biological while gender is a social construct? How can a culture simultaneously

produce scientific medicine like this while claiming that Rachel
Levine and Caitlyn Jenner are women?

Grossman points out the utter hypocrisy and obvious contradiction inherent in trans ideology in her book, *You're Teaching
My Child What?*:

> Take, for example, the hypothetical case of Roberta. She
> feels trapped in the wrong body. Her sex and gender are
> not aligned. She wants bilateral mastectomies, testoster-
> one shots, and other irreversible procedures for relief of
> her distress. Educators have compassion for Roberta's
> plight. Chromosomes don't matter, they say, it's Roberta's
> sense of herself that counts. She is to be called Robert, and
> her right to self-determination is respected. Even if she's
> only thirteen.[33]

To any honest adult, this is disturbing on its face. However,
when you compare it to the way we treat the Ls and the Gs,
the contradictory nature of the acronym becomes unavoidable.
Grossman makes this point by referring to Hector, one of her
patients:

> He's attracted to members of the same sex, but it doesn't
> feel right. It's not who he really is. He chooses to struggle
> against the attraction, and work toward what feels genu-
> ine. But Hector is told he's in denial. You're just refusing to
> accept who you really are, he is told. You must recognize
> your true identity, and stop trying to change the unchange-
> able. Trust us, we know. This is the proper response, say
> educators, even if Hector is forty years old.[34]

CHAPTER 5

The Ubiquitous, Ever-Growing, Self-Contradictory Acronym—Part II

QIA2S+

Aside from the T, the Q—for "queer"—is the most contradictory letter in the acronym.

[B]oth transgenderism and queer theory are predicated on a basic denial of the fixed nature of gender, something that the L and the G by contrast assume. Thus, unlike the L and the G, the T and the Q are transgressive ideologies in the sense that they aim at the demolition of any construction of reality that takes the idea of male and female as representing something that is at root essential.[1]

"Queer" used to be a synonym for "gay," but the advent of queer theory in the 1980s changed all of that. Queer is now an identity without an essence.

Authors Helen Pluckrose and James Lindsay tell us queer theory "is about liberation from the normal, especially where it comes to norms of gender and sexuality. This is because it regards the very existence of categories of sex, gender, and sexuality to be oppressive."[2] At the end of the day, queer theory is a negation of the entire acronym because it

> presumes that oppression follows from categorization, which arises every time language constructs a sense of what is "normal" by producing and maintaining rigid categories of sex (male and female), gender (masculine and feminine), and sexuality (straight, gay, lesbian, bisexual, and so on) and "scripting" people into them. These seemingly straightforward concepts are seen as oppressive, if not violent, and so the main objective of Queer Theory is to examine, question, and subvert them, in order to break them down.[3]

As one queer theorist puts it, "Informed by queer theory, my use of 'queer' is not only meant to register a child's potential desire for same-sex relations or LGBTQ identity but also gestures toward more expansive ways to account for children's deviances from normativity."[4] If you found that sentence hard to cipher, welcome to queer theory. In fact, welcome to the whole set of academic grievance studies. These quasi-academic disciplines disguise their perverse ideas and lack of rigor by using language that, at first glance, sounds sophisticated and academic, but, upon closer examination, reveals a shallow, often shockingly immoral truth that could have been stated with fewer words and far greater clarity. Read a paper on nuclear physics and you may need to look up a few technical terms. Read a paper on queer theory and you will have to unravel unnecessarily complex sentence structures and the use of words whose only purpose is pretense and deception.

The Q vs. the Rest of the Acronym

"There is a frightening new version of homophobia pervading the U.S., disguised as, of all things, 'LGBTQ' activism," writes LGBT activist Ben Appel in *Newsweek*. Recalling an internship he had as an undergraduate, he recalls,

> I was, I quickly learned, not the right kind of "queer." I was just another "cis" (short for "cisgender," a word I had never even heard until it was assigned to me, typically as a slur) gay male—in other words, a privileged and unevolved relic of the past. After all, I had my rights—the right to marry, the right to serve openly in the military, the right to assimilate into this oppressive, "cisheteronormative," patriarchal society. It was time to make way for a new generation of "queer," one that had very little to do with sex-based rights and more to do with abolishing the concepts of sex and sexuality altogether.[5]

Appel came to realize that "[q]ueer theorists insist that subverting the categorizations which have been imposed upon young people . . . is the ultimate expression of autonomy, and further, the key to liberating society from a system devised largely . . .

by cisgender white men."[6] In other words, he learned that the Q was completely at odds with the rest of the acronym.

Christopher Rufo is an investigative reporter whose work has exposed a vast array of neo-Marxist agendas and efforts. He was at the forefront of exposing Black Lives Matter's hypocrisy after its meteoric rise in 2020. He did yeoman's work in exposing Disney's not-so-secret queer agenda to indoctrinate kids through movies and TV shows. But some of his most important work has been in the realm of government education, which leaders of the LGBTQIA2S+ movement have made a concerted effort to infiltrate and influence with modern queer theory. Let's look at a few of the things he's uncovered.

Drag Queen Story Hour

Few stories have caused as much shock and outrage as those about Drag Story Hour (formerly known as Drag Queen Story Hour) have. What many people don't know is that DSH is a recognized 501(c)(3) organization established in San Francisco in 2015.

So what is Drag Story Hour? From the DSH website:

It's just what it sounds like! Storytellers using the art of drag to read books to kids in libraries, schools, and bookstores.

DSH captures the imagination and play of the gender fluidity of childhood and gives kids glamorous, positive, and unabashedly queer role models.

In spaces like this, kids are able to see people who defy rigid gender restrictions and imagine a world where everyone can be their authentic selves![7]

Sexy Sex Ed Camp

In 2021, a nonprofit coalition called Sexy Sex Ed organized a series of "Sexy Summer Camp" events that targeted minors and included lessons on "sex liberation," "gender exploration," "BDSM," "being a sex worker," "self-managed abortions," and "sexual activity while using licit and illicit drugs."[8] The program, according to Rufo,

> is the brainchild of Tanya Turner, who calls herself a "femme, fat, queer, magical pleasure worker" who was raised by "a host of witchy women" in a "coven-like mountain matriarchy" and uses "crystals," "sex toys," and "tarot" in her teaching.[9]

The sessions included "Sex with Me Self-Pleasure Workshop," "Gender Diversity," "Let's Talk About Sex," "Sexy Trans Sex Ed," "The 3 Ps: Pee, Poop, and Pleasure," "Sex on Drugs," and "Eugenics in Appalachia."[10] Remember, this was a summer camp for minors!

Radical Gender Curriculum for Pre-K

In another report, Rufo revealed the following:

> The Evanston–Skokie School District (near Chicago) has adopted a radical gender curriculum that teaches pre-kindergarten through third-grade students to celebrate the transgender flag, break the "gender binary" established by white "colonizers," and experiment with neo-pronouns such as "ze," "zir," and "tree."[11]

In kindergarten, the lessons on gender and trans identity go deeper.

> When we show whether we feel like a boy or a girl or some of each, we are expressing our gender identity. There are also children who feel like a girl and a boy; or like neither a boy or a girl. We can call these children transgender.[12]

Students are expected to be able to "explain the importance of the rainbow flag and trans flag" and are asked to consider their own gender identity.[13]

The Los Angeles Unified School District has adopted a radical gender-theory curriculum instructing teachers to work toward the "breakdown of the gender binary," to experiment with gender pronouns such as "they," "ze," and "tree," and to adopt "trans-affirming" programming to make their classrooms "queer all school year."[14]

> In a week-long conference last fall, titled "Standing with LGBTQ+ Students, Staff, and Families," administrators hosted workshops with presentations on "breaking the [gender] binary," providing children with "free gender affirming clothing," understanding "what your queer middle schooler wants you to know," and producing "counternarratives against the master narrative of mainstream white cis-heteropatriarchy society." The narrative follows the standard academic slop: white, cisgender, heterosexual men have built a repressive social structure, divided the world into the false binary of man and woman, and used this myth to oppress racial and sexual minorities. Religion,

too, is a mechanism of repression. During the conference, the district highlighted how teachers can "respond to religious objections" to gender ideology and promoted materials on how students can be "Muslim and Trans."[15]

The most disturbing story of them all involved the National Education Association's "LGBTQ+ Caucus." They created a website for public school employees that promotes nonbinary identities, a how-to guide for "queer sex," and the idea that "transgender men can get pregnant."[16] The NEA and its local affiliate in Hilliard, Ohio, have been providing staff in the Hilliard City School District with QR code-enabled badges that point to the "NEA LGBTQ+ Caucus" website and resources from gender activist organizations including Scarleteen, Gender Spectrum, The Trevor Project, Teen Health Source, and Sex, Etc.[17] Rufo also was able to obtain a copy of one of the PowerPoint presentations. Its contents are beyond disturbing:

There are some kinds of sex that we hear a lot about. Other kinds of sex, particularly kinds of sex that queer or trans people may be interested in, don't get a lot of coverage. This recipe book is designed to give you more information about some of the sex acts that we think don't get enough play.[18]

The presentation goes on to explain (in disturbing detail) anal sex, bondage, rimming, domination, sadomasochism, sexting, fingering, muffing, outercourse, masturbation, and fisting.[19] Remember, the largest teacher's union in the United States is promoting this. This is what Miriam Grossman had in mind when she wrote, "Sex education is not about health—it's a social movement, a vehicle for changing the world. It happens one child at a time, and it goes on right under your nose."[20]

How did we get here?! Rather than dive into the deep, obscure, and often confusing weeds of academic papers on these subjects, let's examine two very clear and rather explicit essays that go a long way toward answering that question.

Gayle Rubin: Thinking Sex

In her seminal 1987 piece, "Thinking Sex: Notes for a Radical Theory of the Politic of Sexuality," considered by many to be the first primer on queer theory, cultural anthropologist and sexual activist Gayle Rubin reminds us of Alfred Kinsey's broad and lasting influence, writing that

> Alfred Kinsey approached the study of sex with the same uninhibited curiosity he had previously applied to examining a species of wasp. His scientific detachment gave his work a refreshing neutrality that enraged moralists and caused immense controversy.[21]

In her paper, Rubin highlights the experiences of photographer Jacqueline Livingston, which, according to Rubin, "exemplify [what she saw as] the climate created by the child porn panic."[22] Livingston was fired from her teaching position at Cornell University in 1978 after exhibiting pictures of male nudes "which included photographs of her seven-year-old son masturbating."[23] Rubin saw the firing and ensuing fallout—not what Livingston did—as an atrocity:

Ms. magazine, *Chrysalis*, and *Art News* all refused to run ads for Livingston's posters of male nudes. At one point, Kodak confiscated some of her film, and for several months, Livingston lived with the threat of prosecution under the child pornography laws. The Tompkins Country Department of Social Services investigated her fitness as a parent. Livingston's posters have been collected by the Museum of Modern Art, the Metropolitan, and other major museums. But she has paid a high cost in harassment and anxiety for her efforts to capture on film the uncensored male body at different ages.[24]

Rubin repeatedly defends pederasty and pedophilia. She bemoans the fact that

boylovers are so stigmatized that it is difficult to find defenders for their civil liberties, let alone for their erotic orientation.[25]. . . Unfortunately, progressive political analysis of sexuality is relatively underdeveloped. . . . Much of what is available from the feminist movement has simply added to the mystification that shrouds the subject. There is an urgent need to develop radical perspectives on sexuality.[26]

That perspective came to be known as queer theory. Rubin believed that "[S]exuality is impervious to political analysis as long as it is primarily conceived as a biological phenomenon or an aspect of individual psychology." To her, "Sexuality is as much a human product as are diets, methods of transportation, systems of etiquette, forms of labour, types of entertainment, processes of production, and modes of oppression."[27]

Sound familiar? It should. It is the same old neo-Marxist, "social construct" rhetoric. To queer theorists, sexuality is a social construct devised to oppress "sexual minorities," and the only way to fix it is to eradicate it before it takes hold. Hence, they must target children. And the younger the better.

Hannah Dyer: Queer Futurity

I was first introduced to Hannah Dyer's work by New Discourses founder James Lindsay, who spent an entire two-and-a-half-hour podcast analyzing one of her academic journal articles. The podcast was part of a series titled "Groomer Schools," which speaks to the reality of how government schools, with the inclusion of queer ideology, are grooming children to be part of a cult that will make it easier for adult pedophiles to target them. If you are asking yourself, "How could anyone spend two and a half hours analyzing an academic journal article? And why would anyone listen to it?" then you are probably not familiar with queer theory or its influence in modern education.

Dyer's paper, "Queer Futurity and Childhood Innocence: Beyond the Injury of Development," is important for several reasons.[28] First, it appeared in the journal *Global Studies of Childhood*, which means it is not simply the musings of a random academic. Her work represents the mainstream of queer thought. Second, Dyer speaks the quiet part out loud: She says things that many would prefer to hide about the queer movement. Third, her paper is a roadmap for queering education (and explains what that means). Finally, it reveals a clear departure from every aspect of the rest of the acronym.

With that in mind, let us take an unpleasant but necessary journey into a piece that exposes queer theory for the dangerous, contradictory, subversive, and predatory ideology it is:

> Drawing on and deepening recent attempts to meld the fields of childhood studies and queer theory, I dwell on the contradiction that results from the synchronous assumptions of the child's asexuality and proto-heterosexuality to show how emphasizing sexuality within a discussion of children's education is constructive.[29]

This sentence from Dyer's abstract is convoluted, yet revealing. From it we see that she intends to "meld the fields of childhood studies and queer theory." This is disturbing on its face. But it gets worse. She dwells on what she sees as "the contradiction that results from the synchronous assumptions of the child's asexuality and proto-heterosexuality." In plain English, that means she has a problem with the idea that children are either asexual or naturally heterosexual. Finally, she intends to "show how emphasizing sexuality within a discussion of children's education is constructive." This is neo-Marxist code for, "I intend to show that we need to sexualize early childhood education in order to eliminate heteronormativity and sexualize children as early as possible." This is important to Dyer because, "The child has become both a limit and a hope for queer theory."[30] Yes, you read that right. Cue Whitney Houston: "I believe the children are our future . . ."

Key to all of this is Dyer's view that children are wrongly understood to be "innocent." She writes, "There is a paradox that arises when the child's rights to agency and participation in the world are secured while it is suggested that they are innocent and lacking complexity."[31] Dyer sees the innocence of children as mere suggestion or opinion, not reality. She believes "the rhetoric of innocence that envelops normative theories of childhood development has the damaging effect of reducing the child to a figure without complexity."[32] Thus, she hopes to

> illustrate how some of the affective, libidinal, epistemological, and political insistences on childhood innocence can injure the child's development and offer a new mode of analytical inquiry that insists upon embracing the child's queer curiosity and patterns of growth.[33]

Nor is this an isolated, extraordinary opinion. As Dyer notes, "Queer theory is now bursting with debates about the status of the child in relation to futurity, politics, and sexual subjectivity." But since the field of early childhood education largely resists "learning from and carefully attending to these conversations," Dyer believes "there remains a palpable nervousness and discomfort in this field of thought and practice when childhood comes into contact with sexuality."[34] Shame on those early childhood educators who resist the ideas that 1) children are free agents, 2) are not innocent, and 3) these ideas need to be applied to their sexuality!

In the end, Dyer hopes "that a queer methodological approach to child development and education can more generally disrupt teleologically constructed narratives of growth that require a developmental sequence which culminates in normalcy."[35] This can be achieved if queer theorists succeed in their efforts to "queer the rhetoric of innocence that constrains all children and help to refuse attempts to calculate the child's future before it has the opportunity to explore desire."[36] In short, queer theorists not only want to "disrupt" the process of "normal" development—they want to abolish the idea of "normal" altogether, expose children to sexualized queer ideology as early as possible, and celebrate whatever the not-so-innocent children come up with in the end.

The I (the Only Truly Scientific Part of the Acronym)

The I in the acronym stands for intersex. Intersex is also known as "having a difference of sex development," and was previously known as "hermaphrodism" (now considered a stigmatizing and insensitive term).[37] The latest statistics show that 1 in 100 people are intersex.[38] Intersex conditions occur as a result of differences in genetics and hormonal levels in utero. There are as many as thirty variations of intersex.[39]

Intersex individuals exist. They have very real conditions. They also have very real physical, emotional, and spiritual struggles. These are not people who feel trapped in the wrong body or have an "orientation" based on desires or proclivities. Their conditions are objective realities with definable diagnoses. Unfortunately, their inclusion in the so-called "sexual minority acronym" is a ploy to use people's tragic circumstances to score political points.

The A (Exposing the Political Strategy)

The "A" in the acronym stands for Allies. Allies are people who support one or more of the other parts of the acronym, regardless of whether or not they support the others. Do you support the Ls and Gs, but not the Bs or the Ts? No matter, you're an ally. Do you support your child who was born an I, but reject the rest of the acronym as a political ploy to use your child's condition to advance others' political strategies? Too bad, you're an A, and part of the acronym family whether you want to be or not.

However, the biggest impact of adding allies to the acronym can be seen in the schools. Children are being recruited as allies through a consistent barrage of LGBTQIA2S+ material ranging from library books to Drag Queen Story Hour, and an ever-increasing emphasis on queer theory in education. And all of this has approval and support from the highest levels of the education industrial complex, from federal to state and local boards and departments of education. Children are bombarded with this material as early as pre-kindergarten.

The 2S (Their Attempt to Bring in Antiracism and Anticolonialism)

The 2S is the newest addition to the acronym. It stands for two-spirit, which is a term attributed to indigenous peoples of North America. It refers to a person who embodies both male and female spirits, particularly men who identify and dress as women. The *Gender and Sexuality Dictionary* (yes there is such a thing) defines two-spirit as

> a third gender found in some Native American cultures, often involving birth-assigned men or women taking on the identities and roles of the opposite sex. A sacred and historical identity, two-spirit can include but is by no means limited to LGBTQ identities.[40]

The 2S designation is important to the broader movement for at least three reasons. First, it lends credence to the idea that gender is a social construct—at least, as long as you don't look too closely. The argument goes something like this: Before the evil colonizers came to North America, there were peaceful peoples living in harmony with one another and with nature (except when they were slaughtering each other in wars or pagan rituals, but I digress). These people were not bound by the Western, Judeo-Christian idea of the gender binary, as evidenced by the presence of two-spirit individuals.

Of course, the problem is 2S would also have to be a social construct. But I guess as long as it was not constructed by the "white man," that's OK.

Second, 2S is useful to the broader acronym because the designation was given by indigenous North American tribes. Thus, it is free of the baggage that comes along with all things Western Civ. More importantly, it predates colonialism and is thus considered morally superior by virtue of being connected to black, indigenous people of color.

Finally, the 2S designation is impossible for white people to appropriate. The rest of the alphabet is readily available to people of all ethnicities, but 2S is the exclusive domain of tribal peoples of North America.

The + (Their Version of "To an Unknown God")

I can remember when the acronym used to be just LGBT. Then came the "plus." Since then, numerous letters have been added to the ever-growing acronym; that's what the plus has always been about. This is an ever-growing movement. It reminds me of the Apostle Paul's visit to the Areopagus:

So Paul, standing in the midst of the Areopagus, said: "Men of Athens, I perceive that in every way you are very religious. For as I passed along and observed the objects of your worship, I found also an altar with this inscription: 'To the unknown god.' What therefore you worship as unknown, this I proclaim to you." (Acts 17:22–23)

The Athenians were careful to pay homage to "the unknown god" so as not to offend even an unknown deity.[41] In the same way, the plus in the ever-growing acronym is an acknowledgment of and attempt not to offend all the sexual minorities waiting in the wings whose proclivities have yet to be destigmatized. And as soon as that destigmatization happens, the new letters will be welcomed into the acronym and considered to be sexual minorities whose struggle is just like being black.

Dear reader, I hope you see what's happening. We are not *discovering* new sexual minorities; we are witnessing a political power play rooted in the appropriation of the civil rights movement. Author Stephen Baskerville's words ring true:

The Sexual Revolution, it is now apparent, has been about much more than simply discarding sexual inhibitions and restrictions. Like all revolutions, it has been driven from the start by revolutionaries seeking power. . . . Feminists and more recently homosexual political activists . . . have now positioned themselves at the vanguard of left-wing politics, shifting the political discourse from the economic and racial to the social and increasingly the sexual. What was once a socialist campaign against private enterprise and private property has expanded into a social and sexual confrontation with the private family, marriage, masculinity, and religion. This marks a truly new kind of politics, the most personal and thus potentially the most total politics ever devised: the politics of sexual and family life.[42]

The Growth of the Movement

CHAPTER 6

How We Got Here

Tracing the trajectory that brought us to where we are today requires examining two different sources. One source is anti-Christian, neo-Marxist ideology. A second is quasi-Christian subversion.

The anti-Christian, neo-Marxist ideology is rooted in one idea: The world and all the interactions therein can be reduced to power dynamics. All relationships, whether personal, familial, communal, civil, or global, are based on this. There are only those who have power and want to keep it, and those who do not have power and cannot attain it. The reason power remains in the hands of the powerful is cultural hegemony—the domination or rule in a society maintained through ideological or cultural means. It is achieved though social institutions like education, religion, and politics. It allows those in power to influence the values, norms, ideas, expectations, worldview, and behavior of the rest of society.

The key to understanding hegemony is to first understand the underlying assumptions of materialism that inform Marxist thought. From the materialist perspective, there is no absolute truth. There are only socially constructed norms, and whoever constructs those norms does so for the express purpose of ensuring their own power. Hence, in the Christian West, the religious and sociopolitical norms are not right and true because they come from God through the Bible; they come from the Bible in order to give power to those who establish them to subjugate everybody else.

What sinister aspects lie at the bedrock of America's cultural hegemony? What are the values, norms, ideas, expectations, worldview, and behaviors established by the Judeo-Christian worldview to solidify its hegemonic domination of the rest of society? The list of things the wokerati want to overthrow is long, including (but not limited to) rugged individualism ("you get what you work hard for"); the nuclear family (mother, father, and 2.3 children), the scientific method (objective, rational, linear thinking); history (as seen through the lens of the British Empire and Greek, Roman, and Judeo-Christian traditions); Protestant work ethic ("work before play"); religion (especially Christianity as the norm); planning for the future; timeliness; justice (as based on English common law); and competition (when it means there must be winners and losers).

There are so many things wrong with this that it's hard to know where to begin. First, almost everything on this list is a universally accepted norm (like objective, rational, linear thinking and cause-and-effect relationships). Others are more subjective, but make perfect sense. For instance, why would justice in U.S. be based on anything other than English common law, given our status as a former collection of English colonies? Why *wouldn't* U.S. history be based on the primacy of Western

(Greek, Roman) and Judeo-Christian tradition, or U.S. holidays be based on Christian tradition? One wonders how far people would get in life without timeliness, the scientific method, or delayed gratification, to name just a few.

If you're wondering what this has to do with same-sex marriage and other elements of the LGBTQIA2S+ agenda, the answer is *everything*! If Western civilization and its attending morality are merely social constructs designed to ensure the hegemonic power of white, male, cisgendered, heterosexual, able-bodied, native-born people, and biblical-traditional marriage and family are part of that construct, then the thoughtful neo-Marxist (and anyone unwittingly influenced by him) is obligated to problematize and deconstruct that institution. And that is exactly what they are attempting to do.

Not everyone promoting this ideology has done so openly, knowingly, or even recently. A variety of individuals and movements have argued for the rights of so-called "sexual minorities" from a variety of perspectives, in a variety of settings, across many eras. Let's examine a few.

The Civil Rights Movement

When I first set out to write this book, I was convinced that the gay movement of the 1980s and '90s was engaging in a strategy to highjack the civil rights movement of the 1950s and '60s. Then I stumbled upon this quote from civil rights activist Bayard Rustin proving it:

> Today, blacks are no longer the litmus paper or the barometer of social change. Blacks are in every segment of society and there are laws that help to protect them from

racial discrimination. The new "niggers" are gays. . . . It is in this sense that gay people are the new barometer for social change. . . . The question of social change should be framed with the most vulnerable group in mind: gay people.[1]

Rustin was a member of the Communist Party USA and the American Socialist Party. He went to India in the 1940s to study Gandhi's nonviolent tactics. He later met Martin Luther King Jr. in the 1950s and mentored him in nonviolent tactics.[2] He went on to become one of King's leading strategists, advisors, and ghostwriters. He organized the Montgomery bus boycott and spoke at the March on Washington. In other words, Rustin was no outsider to the civil rights movement.

He was also a homosexual. One night in January 1953, hours after giving a speech in Pasadena, California, Rustin was spotted in a parked car, having sex with two other men. He was sentenced to sixty days in jail and forced to register as a sex offender.[3]

King was well aware of Rustin's homosexuality, as well as his tendency to mingle black social justice with gay social justice. King agreed with another close advisor/ghostwriter, Stanley Levinson, that the race issue should be the priority: Homosexuality was not to be conflated during the climactic point of the civil rights movement in the 1960s. King and Levinson also agreed that Rustin and fellow civil rights activist James Baldwin were more qualified to lead a homosexual movement. So it is not the case that the homosexual movement suddenly decided to hitch its wagon to another successful movement after the fact. The two movements were very much intertwined

as far back as the 1950s—and what united them was a commitment to neo-Marxist ideals.

What Does This Mean for You?

I described in some detail in chapter three how Marshall Kirk and
Hunter Madsen teamed up in 1989 to write *After the Ball: How
America Will Overcome Its Fear and Hatred of Gays in the 90s.*
AIDS was rampant at the time, and people were blaming homosexuals for it. I am noting again here that Lillian Faderman captured the homosexual perspective on that period in her critically
acclaimed book, *The Gay Revolution: The Story of the Struggle*:

> The Far Right did not waste the shock value.
> Paleoconservative Patrick Buchanan gloated in his syn-
> dicated column that AIDS was a sign that "Nature is
> exacting retribution"; but now, he wrote, not only were
> these homosexuals a "moral menace," they were a "public
> health menace," too. Buchanan reported that policemen
> were so worried about getting AIDS and bringing it home
> to their families that they had to don masks and gloves
> when dealing with homosexual lawbreakers; landlords
> were so worried about the spread of AIDS on their prem-
> ises that they had to evict infected homosexuals from their
> property. Because of homosexuals' morally irresponsible
> and unhealthy sex practices, they were the spreaders of a
> host of other diseases, too, that could affect innocent het-
> erosexuals, such as hepatitis. Therefore, Buchanan ranted,
> they must not be allowed to work in restaurants or any job
> in which they handled food. "Gay rights"—homosexuals'

demands to live and work wherever they wanted—were dangerous to heterosexuals.[4]

In the midst of all the furor over AIDS, Kirk and Madsen hatched a plan to turn the tables, which I also laid out for you in chapter three. Here's what they said about it at the time:

> AIDS, though a loose cannon, is a cannon indeed. As cynical as it may seem, AIDS gives us a chance, however brief, to establish ourselves as a victimized minority legitimately deserving of America's special protection and care. This, therefore, is the question and the challenge: how can we surmount our "insurmountable" opportunity? How can we maximize the sympathy and minimize the fear? How, given the horrid hand that AIDS has dealt us, can we best play it?[5]

One of the inevitable consequences of the "gay is the new black" paradigm is the eventual elimination of religious freedom protections. In late 2022, Senator Mitt Romney (R-UT) and other congressional Republicans justified their support of the "Respect for Marriage Act"—which protects same-sex marriages nationwide from federal nullification even if the U.S. Supreme Court someday overturns *Obergefell*—by denying this inevitable reality. "While I believe in traditional marriage," Romney said, "*Obergefell* is and has been the law of the land upon which LGBTQ individuals have relied. This legislation provides certainty to many LGBTQ Americans, and it signals that Congress—and I—esteem and love all of our fellow Americans equally."[6]

Romney made these remarks as a compromise after Republican senators Susan Collins from Maine and Thom Tillis from North Carolina, as well as Democrat senators Tammy Baldwin from Wisconsin and Kyrsten Sinema from Arizona, added a "bipartisan amendment to "strengthen religious liberty protections in the bill."[7]

However, this is naïve at best. If it is true that homosexuality is as innate and immutable as race, and forbidding same-sex marriage is tantamount to antimiscegenation, then it must follow that allowing the Church to discriminate against same-sex marriage is as morally reprehensible as *Loving v. Virginia*. At the time of this writing, all public institutions are required to recognize same-sex marriage in their policies; though private institutions have been spared so far, it can't remain that way for long. The day will come when the full weight of the law will be brought to bear on churches that hold to a biblical view of marriage to obey man's law rather than God's law.

The Execution of the Strategy

Earlier, I touched briefly on a few points showing how far LGBTQIA2S+ activists have come in achieving the agenda first laid out by Kirk and Madsen in 1989. Here are a few more details.

How Have They Done with Desensitizing?

"Drag queen, LGBT fans star alongside Serena Williams and Ukraine in new ESPN ad." So read a headline on OutSports. com. The piece notes, "ESPN features the LGBT community and the Pride rainbow in inclusive commercial for the sports network."[8]

Remember, the goal of the desensitization step in their strategy was to get straight people so used to seeing homosexuals in the media that they were no longer affected by it.

By 2020, Wikipedia had a list of some eighty TV shows with gay characters.[9] Anyone who watches a significant amount of television knows that nowadays, it would be easier to name shows that *do not* have a gay character. I've heard it said that if a future anthropologist had only our television shows as evidence, he would believe most of us are gay or trans and almost no one is a Christian.

How Have They Done with Jamming?

What if I told you I went to a church and the pastor stood behind the pulpit and started his sermon like this:

"My topic today is adultery. But before I begin, let me state clearly that I love adulterers. Jesus loves adulterers. I have several friends who are actively engaged in adultery. I think it is important that we make it clear that, even though the Bible speaks against adultery, it does not speak against adulterers. Many adulterers have been hurt by the Church's harsh rhetoric about adultery. Many adulterers don't want to have anything to do with the Church because of our rhetoric, and that is terrible witness."

Have you ever heard anything like that before? If you've heard a sermon on homosexuality in the last few years, you've probably heard something *exactly* like that. Sermons on homosexuality these days die the death of a thousand qualifications, not because the Bible gives special status to the sin of homosexuality, but because we have been jammed!

Perhaps the clearest cases of jamming have come when prominent Christians have been put on the spot in the media. Let's look at a few.

Joel Osteen:

The pastor of the largest church in America, Joel Osteen, is one of Oprah Winfrey's favorite preachers. In 2012, Osteen told Oprah he thinks homosexuals will go to heaven.[10] He had already admitted to talk-show host Piers Morgan that he only talks about homosexuality during interviews and never addresses it from the pulpit.[11] On CNN, he said he "tries to stay in his lane, that he just wants to encourage people to be better." He also reiterated that he only talks about this during interviews.[12]

Carl Lentz:

Lentz was the pastor of Hillsong NYC in New York before his very public moral failure ousted him from the pulpit in late 2020. Lentz sat down for a television for an interview with Katie Couric in June 2014, a testament to Lentz's and Hillsong's massive popularity. "We have a stance on love; everything else, we have conversations," he told Couric. When she pressed him on the issue of same-sex marriage, Lentz dodged the question and said, "Very rarely did Jesus ever talk about morality or social issues. He was about the deeper things of the heart."[13]

T. D. Jakes:

Jakes, perhaps the most well-known preacher in America besides Osteen, sat down with Marc Lamont Hill on his TV show in 2015. Hill broached the subject of homosexuality by reading a question from a viewer who asked, "Do you [think] the LGBT community and the black church can coexist?" Without hesitation or equivocation, Jakes responded, "Absolutely!" Hill pressed the issue and Jakes went on a meandering rant about no two churches being the same and no two LGBT people being the same and that people need to find churches that agree with their views. When Hill asked Jakes if his views on homosexuality had evolved, Jakes responded, "Evolved and evolving . . . We bought into the myth that this was a Christian nation, and once you get past that . . . Once you begin to understand that a republic is designed to be an overarching system to protect our unique nuances, then we no longer look for public policy to reflect biblical ethics." Hill then went on to use the well-worn trope that "the Church has changed on slavery due to changing views . . ." to press Jakes on his hermeneutical understanding of the subject. Jakes ended up stating, "It's a complex issue."[14]

At the end of the day, these responses are all evidence of jamming. The LGBTQ+ movement has successfully equated opposition to homosexuality or same-sex marriage with the most heinous individuals, groups, and episodes in history. Being against any of the things that movement now advocates is viewed as the equivalent of being a Nazi skinhead.

How Have They Done with Conversion?

The political landscape in the United States and across the West has changed dramatically in this century concerning marriage. A quick look at the positions taken by three U.S. presidents—Bill Clinton, Barack Obama, and Joe Biden—puts that change in stark relief. All of them flipped on this issue over time—and sometimes more than once:

- Bill Clinton went from signing the "Don't Ask, Don't Tell" policy—allowing homosexuals to serve in the military as long as they stayed closeted—in 1993 to urging his adopted home state of New York to legalize same-sex marriage in 2011. In the interim, he told *The Advocate* in 1996, "I remain opposed to same-sex marriage. I believe marriage is an institution for the union of a man and a woman. *This has been my long-standing position, and it is not being reviewed or considered*"[15]—and backed that up by signing the Defense of Marriage Act into law later that year.

- Barack Obama stated he was "unequivocally" for same-sex marriage when he was running for the Illinois Senate in 2006,[16] but just two years later, publicly stated, "I believe marriage is between a man and a woman. I am not in favor of gay marriage."[17] By 2012, he was trying to split the difference by saying he personally believes same-sex marriage should be allowed, but that the matter should be decided on the state level, not federal.[18] But once he was elected president, the gloves came off. In his inaugural address in 2012, he said, "Our journey is not complete until our gay brothers and sisters are treated like anyone else under the law—for if we are truly created equal, then surely the love we commit to one another must be equal as well."[19] During his second term, his administration failed to defend DOMA, paving the way for *Obergefell* in 2015.

- As a U.S. senator in 1994, Joe Biden voted to withhold federal funding from schools that portrayed homosexuality "as a positive lifestyle," distributed materials portraying homosexuality in this way, or referred students

"to an organization that affirms a homosexual lifestyle."[20] In 1996, he voted for DOMA, which blocked the
federal government from recognizing same-sex marriages.[21] In 2006, before becoming Obama's running mate
and subsequent vice president, Biden was unequivocal in
his opposition to same-sex marriage, saying that since
DOMA was already the law of the land, there was no
need for a constitutional amendment enshrining the biblical definition of marriage.[22]

But by 2012, Biden had done a complete 180, stating, "Men
marrying men, women marrying women, and heterosexual men
and women marrying another are entitled to the same exact
rights, all the civil rights, all the civil liberties. And quite frankly,
I don't see much of a distinction beyond that."[23] He also lied
about supporting DOMA, saying, "I cast a vote against the
so-called Defense of Marriage Act, which was a homophobic act
brought by the right wing."[24]

And, of course, after ascending to the presidency in 2020, he
has done everything in his power to support the LGBTQIA2S+
agenda—from his unconditional support for transitioning
minors from one gender to another and appointing the first
openly transgender person to a cabinet position to flying the
rainbow flag and holding a Pride Month celebration at the White
House to threatening to withhold federal funding from Uganda
in retaliation for passing an anti-homosexuality bill in 2023.[25]

Honorable Mention: Donald Trump
At the time of his inauguration, Donald Trump had the distinction of being "the only president to take office supporting gay

marriage."[26] His statements on same-sex marriage are far less definitive than his predecessors' and thus harder to characterize as flip-flops. Nevertheless, when compared to the Republican Party Platform, and in light of the clear battle lines drawn on the issue, it is clear that Trump is not a stalwart on marriage. In a 2015 interview with CNN's Jake Tapper, Trump at least did enough to calm the fears of conservatives when he said he was "in favor of traditional marriage."[27]

After the Supreme Court handed down the *Obergefell* decision in 2015, Trump told Howard Kurtz he would have preferred for the court to have left states to make their own decisions and suggested that overturning the ruling was not a priority.[28] He also told *The Hollywood Reporter* it was a "dead issue."[29] But in January 2016, before the Iowa caucuses, he told Chris Wallace that he would "strongly consider" appointing justices who would overturn the *Obergefell* ruling.[30]

In a campaign ad released on Twitter in August 2020, National Intelligence Director Richard Grenell made a claim echoed by many. He said Trump was the "most pro-gay president in history."[31] This was significant coming from the man Trump made America's first openly gay cabinet member.

Giving such a profoundly significant job to an LGBT person was Trump's way of sending two signals to the power brokers in American politics. First, to all observers, this showed that his was an accepting administration that did not see LGBT people as tokens given insignificant jobs for appearance's sake. The second was a more direct message to the establishment Republican Party: Business as usual under previous party leaders—the kind who allowed casual, unchallenged discrimination against LGBT people—was over, for good.[32] During his 2020 presidential campaign, Trump sent Grenell to a dozen "Trump Pride" events between February and May in battleground states including Florida, Pennsylvania, Michigan, and North Carolina. Grenell also leveraged his position to lead State Department initiatives to pressure nations to decriminalize homosexuality.[33]

In another ad for the Log Cabin Republicans, Melania Trump said, "I was shocked to discover that some of these powerful people have tried to paint my husband as anti-gay or against equality. Nothing could be further from the truth."[34] The president confirmed this in his own words in an interview with Fox News's Steve Hilton during the 2016 primary:

> STEVE HILTON: Just one thing on [Pete Buttigieg], putting aside policy disagreements, don't you think it's just great to see that you've got a guy there on the stage with his husband and it's normal—
> TRUMP: I think it's absolutely fine; I do.
> HILTON: But isn't it a sign of great progress in the country that that's just—
> TRUMP: Yeah, I think it's great. I think that's something that perhaps some people will have a problem with. I have no problem with it whatsoever, I think it's good.[35]

It appears Politico was right in proclaiming, "The GOP waves white flag in the same-sex marriage wars."[36] Today it is considered political suicide for anyone running for national office to openly oppose same-sex marriage. One wonders if the same will someday hold true for taking positions that oppose "gender-affirming care" for children.

CHAPTER 7

The Enemy Within

One of the most difficult aspects of this cultural upheaval is the presence of enemies within our camp. These enemies take many forms. Some are nominal Christians, others are non-Christians purporting to speak for Christians by offering their interpretation of the Bible and Christianity. However, they all employ three main tactics, which I will address in this chapter. My goal here is not to give an exhaustive treatment of them, but to make you aware of them, help you see through them, and give you answers to the questions they raise.

Tactic #1: "The Law of Love"

The first tactic is to redefine love, then make that the foundation upon which the message of Christ is built. That new "gospel" serves as justification for same-sex relationships. There are myriad examples of this. Let's look at one from the Huffington Post.

> Jesus calls us to have empathy, compassion and an open heart for all human beings. Not just people who follow

Him. Not just Christians. Not just believers. Not just straight people. BUT EVERYONE. And this includes gay people. They are your neighbors, too. So if we are to follow what Jesus is asking of us, we MUST demand that gay people have the right to marry. Why? Because to NOT do so would not be loving them as we love ourselves. And that would make us hypocrites pretending to love Jesus.[1] (emphasis his)

Note that Kipp does not start with the argument that marriage should be granted to those who "love one another." Instead, he begins by charging Christians who fail to "demand that gay people have the right to marry" with hypocrisy because "Jesus was all about Love, not rules and regulations. But LOVE" (emphasis his).[2] Ironically, Kipp roots his argument in Jesus's summary of the Mosaic Law—that the two greatest commandments are to love God first, and our neighbors as ourselves. Therefore, he concludes "that Jesus would support gay people getting married."[3]

This argument is all too common—and marvelous for at least three reasons. First, it lets us know how the culture sees this issue. Second, it proves my point that the Bible is relevant to the cultural debate. Even HuffPo agrees it is legitimate to consult the Bible about it. Third, it provides us an opportunity to "always [be] prepared to make a defense to anyone who asks you for a reason for the hope that is in you" (1 Peter 3:15). With that in mind, let us offer a defense.

The fact that the broader culture 1) is aware of the Great Commandments, 2) believes they are among the most important words Jesus spoke, and 3) agrees that they carry moral weight and authority represents a great opportunity. If we can demonstrate that these words far from legitimizing same-sex marriage, actually militate against it, those using these arguments will be forced to admit they are wrong, stop using this argument, or (more likely) acknowledge that they don't really care what Jesus actually meant; they are just employing their own version of a "clobber passage." In either case, we have gained ground. More importantly, engaging this argument opens a door to sharing the Gospel.

True Love Is Governed by the Law

The words in question are found in Matthew's gospel:

> But when the Pharisees heard that he had silenced the Sadducees, they gathered together. And one of them, a lawyer, asked him a question to test him. "Teacher, which is the great commandment in the Law?" And he said to him, "You shall love the Lord your God with all your heart and with all your soul and with all your mind. This is the great and first commandment. And a second is like it: You shall love your neighbor as yourself. On these two commandments depend all the Law and the Prophets." (Matthew 22:34–40)

A quick and honest assessment of this text makes several things apparent. First, the question came from a lawyer. Second, the Pharisees were questioning Jesus about the Decalogue (the Ten Commandments). Third, Jesus responds with a statement that, at first glance, appears to avoid the actual question. However, a closer look reveals that Jesus, far from evading, avoiding, or condemning the Decalogue, actually affirmed it!

The Decalogue is divided into two tables. The first four commandments express our duty to God. The last six commandments express our duty to our fellow man. Another way to look at it is the first table is vertical and the second is horizontal, and each were often summarized. The summary of the first table is, "Love the Lord your God with all your heart, soul, mind, and strength," and the second table is, "Love your neighbor as yourself."

The Apostle Paul confirms this:

> Owe no one anything, except to love each other, for the one who loves another has fulfilled the law. For the commandments, "You shall not commit adultery, You shall not murder, You shall not steal, You shall not covet," and any other commandment, are summed up in this word: "You shall love your neighbor as yourself." Love does no wrong to a neighbor; therefore love is the fulfilling of the law. (Romans 13:8–10)

Paul makes it clear that he is referring to the Decalogue by enumerating several of the commandments from the second table. Then he quotes Leviticus 19:18 as a summary of it (see also Galatians 5:14 and James 2:8). This is important because it puts to rest the idea that Jesus's summary of the Law was somehow meant to replace the old, outdated, and oppressive Law of Moses. On the contrary, He actually said earlier:

> "Do not think that I have come to abolish the Law or the Prophets; I have not come to abolish them but to fulfill them. For truly, I say to you, until heaven and earth pass away, not an iota, not a dot, will pass from the Law until all is accomplished. Therefore whoever relaxes one of the least

of these commandments and teaches others to do the same will be called least in the kingdom of heaven, but whoever does them and teaches them will be called great in the kingdom of heaven. For I tell you, unless your righteousness exceeds that of the scribes and Pharisees, you will never enter the kingdom of heaven." (Matthew 5:17–20)

As to how to define "love": One of the most oft-quoted verses in the Bible concerning love is found in 1 Corinthians 13. Ironically, it is most often quoted at weddings. Of particular interest for our purposes are verses 4–6:

Love is patient and kind; love does not envy or boast; it is not arrogant or rude. It does not insist on its own way; it is not irritable or resentful; it does not rejoice at wrongdoing, but rejoices with the truth. (1 Corinthians 13:4–6)

Two things here stand out in relation to our discussion: love "does not insist on its own way" and "does not rejoice at wrongdoing." This ties directly back to the aforementioned passage in that the Law of God defines "wrongdoing."

This sentiment not limited to Paul (a favorite target of the Left, as we shall see shortly). The Psalmist writes, "O you who love the LORD, hate evil! He preserves the lives of his saints; he delivers them from the hand of the wicked" (Psalm 97:10). Paul quotes and expands on this when he writes,

Let love be genuine. Abhor what is evil; hold fast to what is good. Love one another with brotherly affection. Outdo one another in showing honor. (Romans 12:9–10)

Again, love—true, biblical love—is not to be divorced from or pitted against the righteousness of God's Law.

Interestingly, the HuffPo author acknowledges this when he concludes that, regarding "two consenting adults who want to get married,"

> If we love Jesus, if we call ourselves a Christian, then we must follow these top two commandments above all else and rise to the occasion so that every consenting adult has the right to Love and be Loved as they please.[4]

Kipp not only presses the command of the law in theological terms (i.e., if we love Jesus, we *must follow these top two commandments above all else*), he also presses it in civil terms. He argues for this law of love to be applied *with limits*. As it turns out, Kipp believes that Christ's followers are obligated to allow same-sex marriage, but draws the line at polyamory (multiple spouses within a marriage), forced marriage, and marriage between adults and children. So there *are* moral laws we are required to follow.

True Love Calls the Wicked to Repent

Another important feature of biblical love as it relates to this discussion is the fact that the Left sees a contradiction between being loving and calling sinners to repent. Discussions with the "Law of Love" crowd tend to center around the idea that Jesus was all love and no law and that, as a result, those who focus on things like sin are at odds with the true teaching He came to bring. However, the message of the Bible is clear: Watching sinners live in rebellion to God without calling them to repent is, in fact, unloving.

"If I say to the wicked, 'You shall surely die,' and you give him no warning, nor speak to warn the wicked from his wicked way, in order to save his life, that wicked person shall die for his iniquity, but his blood I will require at your hand." (Ezekiel 3:18)

An important point here is that those making the "Law of Love" argument are doing the very thing for which they condemn us: They are saying that we are in sin and contradicting the teaching of our Lord and Savior. They are calling us to repent for violating the law of love while arguing that it militates against calling people to repentance.

Of course, our hope is that answering these objections will help others see 1) that we are not being arbitrary, 2) that we are not twisting or misrepresenting Jesus's teachings, and 3) that we are, in fact, showing love.

Tactic #2: The "Clobber Passage" Sleight of Hand

The second tactic is to take on the so-called "clobber passages"—six key Bible passages that specifically proscribe homosexuality. This tactic is attractive in that it takes on the appearance of being serious about the Bible and interpreting it rightly, giving the appearance of conservative evangelicalism. One of the most important books in this genre is Matthew Vines's *God and the Gay Christian*, which hit the Christian community like a meteor.

Vines struck a chord that resonated among Christians in ways the "Law of Love" crowd could not because he was doing serious exegesis as one who believed in the authority of Scripture. "To be fair," he writes, many Christians now support same-sex relationships. But those who do tend to see Scripture as a helpful but dated guidebook, not as the final authority on questions of morality and doctrine. That is not my view of Scripture. . . . I believe all of Scripture is inspired by God and authoritative for my life.[5]

In taking on the "clobber passages," Vines acknowledges that he is "not a biblical scholar" and therefore "relied on the work of dozens of scholars whose expertise is far greater than my own."[6] My goal here is not to refute his interpretation of these passages, but to focus on the underlying assumptions behind the anti-clobber passage approach.

The Reverend Dr. Marcia Ledford, Esq., "a practical theologian and Episcopal priest,"[7] advocates applying biblical truth to public policy. On her website, she asserts,

We the people of faith, in order to form a more perfect union . . . have First Amendments [sic] rights that protect us in speaking out against unjust laws and policies. We are even protected in speaking in the public square about our faith. We the people of faith must speak out when our government marginalizes people.[8]

Obviously, I welcome this.

Ledford worked as a civil rights attorney for over thirty years, including time with the American Civil Liberties Union, and is dedicated to equipping people to advance the anti-clobber passage argument in practical ways. Consequently, she offers us an opportunity to interact with a succinct, orderly presentation of the argument. She offers a series of talking points:

#1: Paul never knew Jesus personally.

He never experienced Jesus' gentleness and compassion, his healings, and advocacy for sinners, and his love for humanity (Ledford writes). Paul only knew of Jesus from others. He never seemed to understand the importance of Jesus' world-altering love, mercy and forgiveness. Paul would also have been upset and critical that Jesus broke these moral codes of conduct regarding eating.[9]

The best response to this is the Scriptures themselves:

But when Cephas [Peter] came to Antioch, I opposed him to his face, because he stood condemned. For before certain men came from James, he was eating with the Gentiles; but when they came he drew back and separated himself, fearing the circumcision party. And the rest of the Jews acted hypocritically along with him, so that even Barnabas was led astray by their hypocrisy. But when I saw that their conduct was not in step with the truth of the gospel, I said to Cephas before them all, "If you, though a Jew, live like a Gentile and not like a Jew, how can you force the Gentiles to live like Jews?" (Galatians 2:11–14)

How can anyone argue that "Paul would also have been upset and critical that Jesus broke these moral codes of conduct

regarding eating" in light of this passage that proves the opposite, conclusively?

#2: Paul would have had a hard time with Jesus removing the cultic requirements of the cleansing bath or making a sacrifice of thanksgiving.

Why? (Ledford writes) I submit that's because Paul ini-
tially persecuted Christians as Saul, and even oversaw the
stoning of our first martyr, Stephen. Paul revealed his per-
sonality as accuser and prosecutor when he hunted down
Christians and arrested them. His passion continued even
beyond his conversion at Damascus. Paul merely shifted
to criticizing Gentiles–he did not lose his zeal for critiqu-
ing others. Keep this in mind as we work through these
passages.[10]

Again, Ledford shows complete ignorance of the Scriptures!
Otherwise, she would have known Paul's own response to such
criticisms:

But whatever gain I had, I counted as loss for the sake of
Christ. Indeed, I count everything as loss because of the
surpassing worth of knowing Christ Jesus my Lord. For
his sake I have suffered the loss of all things and count
them as rubbish, in order that I may gain Christ and
be found in him, not having a righteousness of my own
that comes from the law, but that which comes through
faith in Christ, the righteousness from God that depends
on faith—that I may know him and the power of his

resurrection, and may share his sufferings, becoming like him in his death, that by any means possible I may attain the resurrection from the dead. (Philippians 3:7–11)

#3: Paul had a heterosexist perspective.

Paul undoubtedly wrote his letters with a heterosexist perspective, and theologians have continued this built-in prejudice even to current times. . . . The idea of desiring to be penetrated causes a negative gut reaction even today… because misogyny, hatred of, or aversion to women and girls is the root cause of homophobic and heterosexist perspectives.[11]

Again, Paul's own words are his best defense against such an attack:

Husbands, love your wives, as Christ loved the church and gave himself up for her, that he might sanctify her, having cleansed her by the washing of water with the word, so that he might present the church to himself in splendor, without spot or wrinkle or any such thing, that she might be holy and without blemish. In the same way husbands should love their wives as their own bodies. He who loves his wife loves himself. For no one ever hated his own flesh, but nourishes and cherishes it, just as Christ does the church, because we are members of his body. (Ephesians 5:25–30)

#4: Paul has a problem with homosexual behavior.

Notice how Paul clusters murderers with gossips, and liars with slave-traders, or kidnappers. And Paul has many other lists that do the same thing. To pair the act of two consenting men in private conduct with murderers and kidnappers would hardly seem balanced in a contemporary reading.

Paul could have been writing about the system of Greek pederasty. This was an erotic relationship that included having sex with the boy, also known as a calamite or *malakoi* (meaning soft, effeminate). Being a Jew, Paul would have been opposed to this Gentile practice and would have had concern for the boys involved.[12]

Like all those who take this tack, Ledford fails to account for Paul's key teaching on the subject where he addresses the fact that "their women exchanged natural relations for those that are contrary to nature" (Romans 1:26)—which proves he's not talking about pederasty.

Nor is Ledford alone on this point. "I'm not saying gay people didn't exist in ancient societies," writes Vines. "I'm simply pointing out that ancient societies didn't think in terms of exclusive sexual orientations." And he is absolutely correct. The idea of "sexual orientation" is recent invention. No one living before the modern era would have heard of it. Vines goes on to add:

In ancient Greece, the most common form of same-sex behavior was something modern societies would never accept: a sexual relationship between a man and an adolescent boy, called pederasty.[13]

Vines is both wrong and naïve. He is wrong because there are societies that accept pederasty today. During the war in Afghanistan, Western soldiers were shocked to learn that many Afghans practiced pederasty—and in fact, some of our troops were disciplined for interfering with the practice.[14] In a disturbing piece titled *Afghanistan's Dirty Little Secret*, we find that

> For centuries, Afghan men have taken boys, roughly 9 to 15 years old, as lovers. . . . Some research suggests that half the Pashtun tribal members in Kandahar and other southern towns are *bacha baz*, the term for an older man with a boy lover.[15]

In fact, there is even a catchphrase that summarizes the practice: "Women are for babies, boys are for pleasure."[16]

Furthermore, Vines is naïve to think that a practice many people find unthinkable today will remain unthinkable tomorrow. He could have said the same thing about same-sex marriage just a generation ago! In fact, we're already there. As noted earlier, we're already seeing a push to change the terminology for pedophiles to "minor-attracted persons" and grooming our youth to promote intergenerational sex and people identifying as things like mermaids and unicorns.

Tactic #3: Why Pick and Choose?

"You shall not lie with a male as with a woman; it is an abomination." So reads Leviticus 18:22. Many Christians avoid quoting this verse, not because the text is unclear, but because doing so invites the inevitable retort, "What about shellfish?" Vines could not resist this line of argumentation in *God and the Gay Christian.*

> Leviticus prohibits male same-sex relations, but it uses similar language to prohibit the eating of shellfish. . . . Yet Christians no longer regard eating shellfish . . . as sinful. . . . A more comprehensive exploration of Scripture is in order.[17]

I could not agree more!

Vines notes that when the Church grew to include Gentiles, the Jewish leaders had to make some important decisions about how much of the Mosaic law to include and "recognized that the old law was no longer binding."[18]

In a classic episode from the second season of *The West Wing* (December 2000), President Jedidiah Bartlett's character, played by Martin Sheen, obliterates a famous radio talk show host who insists on calling homosexuality an abomination. Many on the Left see this as a classic example of pro-homosexual defeat of the "clobber passages." Here's how it plays out:

> BARTLETT: I'm interested in selling my youngest daughter into slavery as sanctioned in Exodus 21:7. She's a Georgetown sophomore, speaks fluent Italian, always cleaned the table when it was her turn. What would a good price for her be?
>
> My chief of staff, Leo McGarrity, insists on working on the Sabbath. Exodus 35:2 clearly says he should be put

to death. Am I morally obligated to kill him myself or is it okay to call the police?

Here's one that's really important, cause we've got a lot of sports fans in this town: touching the skin of a dead pig makes one unclean—Leviticus 11:7. If they promise to wear gloves, can the Washington Redskins still play football? Can Notre Dame? Can West Point?

Does the whole town really have to be together to stone my brother, John, for planting different crops side by side? Can I burn my mother in a small family gathering for wearing garments made from two different threads?

Think about those questions, would you?[19]

The episode was a hit! Gay groups lauded its brilliance. I could list dozens of examples like this, but you get the point. These arguments were not made in academia or on fringe websites or podcasts; they were front and center on primetime TV because they are ground zero in the war to win people's hearts and minds.

Television shows are fiercely competitive and woefully unoriginal. Before something makes it to the air, it has usually been tested, studied, polled, evaluated, and reevaluated in an effort to score points with the target audience. The goal is not to alienate, but to captivate. Hence, *The West Wing* and myriad cultural examples like it demonstrate that many people believe these arguments.

Second, the public and consistent nature of these attacks means they work. And if arguments work, they will show up in multiple arenas until they become common fare among those striving to score points in this and other debates.

Third, these attacks bring the fight to our front door by arguing *from Scripture*. They're basically saying our hermeneutic is to blame. In other words, they are not arguing against the Bible, they are arguing against the way we *interpret* the Bible. This, in fact, is the next front in the battle for biblical truth in the area of sexuality. The rise of the "gay Christian" movement was a harbinger of what we're seeing now.

The Threefold Division of the Law

The quick and dirty response to "the clobber passage" approach is the threefold division of the Law, which is not some fringe doctrine that can be ignored.

There are three types of law: civil (or judicial), ceremonial, and moral.

- The civil law was given to Israel to govern them as a nation in the ancient Near East.
- The ceremonial law was given to Israel to govern their worship, and pointed to the coming of Christ.
- The moral law, given and summarized in the Decalogue, is the timeless, transcendent law of God that governs all men in all places and at all times.

Understanding these three types of law is key to applying them appropriately.

This is a critical point. Even if people disagree with the three-fold division of the law, an honest critic must acknowledge the fact that New Testament Christians are not obligated to keep the ceremonial law. Moreover, since the ceremonial law prefigured

Christ, keeping it would not only be unnecessary, but blasphemous. Paul addresses this specifically:

> Therefore let no one pass judgment on you in questions of food and drink, or with regard to a festival or a new moon or a Sabbath. These are a shadow of the things to come, but the substance belongs to Christ. Let no one disqualify you, insisting on asceticism and worship of angels, going on in detail about visions, puffed up without reason by his sensuous mind, and not holding fast to the Head, from whom the whole body, nourished and knit together through its joints and ligaments, grows with a growth that is from God. If with Christ you died to the elemental spirits of the world, why, as if you were still alive in the world, do you submit to regulations—"Do not handle, Do not taste, Do not touch" (referring to things that all perish as they are used)—according to human precepts and teachings? These have indeed an appearance of wisdom in promoting self-made religion and asceticism and severity to the body, but they are of no value in stopping the indulgence of the flesh. (Colossians 2:16–23)

Likewise, the civil (or judicial) laws of Israel came with an expiration date that ran out when Jesus showed up. The Second London Baptist Confession states:

> To them also he gave sundry judicial Laws, which expired together with the state of that people, not obliging any now by virtue of that institution; their general equity only, being of moral use.

Note that the judicial laws in the Bible are said to have "expired together with the state of that people." In other words, we don't just drag and drop a judicial law from Israel into our judicial law—but that doesn't mean they are completely irrelevant. Since they are predicated on the moral law, they are useful in terms of their "general equity." We see this principle at work in the New Testament. For example, the Old Testament contains several judicial laws related to sexual purity:

> But if the thing is true, that evidence of virginity was not found in the young woman, then they shall bring out the young woman to the door of her father's house, and the men of her city shall stone her to death with stones, because she has done an outrageous thing in Israel by whoring in her father's house. So you shall purge the evil from your midst.
>
> If a man is found lying with the wife of another man, both of them shall die, the man who lay with the woman, and the woman. So you shall purge the evil from Israel. (Deuteronomy 22:20–22; see also Deuteronomy 13:5; 17:7, 12; 21:21)

While New Testament writers don't drag and drop these laws, they do apply their general equity:

> I wrote to you in my letter not to associate with sexually immoral people—not at all meaning the sexually immoral of this world, or the greedy and swindlers, or idolaters, since then you would need to go out of the world. But now I am writing to you not to associate with anyone who

bears the name of brother if he is guilty of sexual immorality or greed, or is an idolater, reviler, drunkard, or swin-
dler—not even to eat with such a one. For what have I to
do with judging outsiders? Is it not those inside the church
whom you are to judge? God judges those outside. "Purge
the evil person from among you." (1 Corinthians 5:9–13)

Note that Paul uses the same idea of "purging the evil" that
we saw in Deuteronomy. Here, he acknowledges the universal,
transcendent nature of the moral law regarding sexual sin but
applies it in a setting that is different from Israel's ancient theo-
cratic government.

The third category of laws in the Bible is the transcendent,
unchanging, and universal moral law.

The moral Law doth for ever bind all, as well justified
persons as others, to the obedience thereof, and that not
only in regard of the matter contained in it, but also in
respect of the authority of God the Creator; who gave it:
Neither doth Christ in the Gospel any way dissolve, but
much strengthen this obligation. (2LBC XIX.5)

This is the same principle we see in works like *Blackstone's
Commentary on the Laws of England*, which was the second
most popular book in colonial America (second only to the
Bible). Blackstone wrote:

MAN, considered as a creature, must necessarily be subject to the laws of his creator, for he is entirely a dependent
being. A being, independent of any other, has no rule to

pursue, but such as he prescribes to himself; but a state of dependance will inevitably oblige the inferior to take the will of him, on whom he depends, as the rule of his conduct: not indeed in every particular, but in all those points wherein his dependence consists. This principle therefore has more or less extent and effect, in proportion as the superiority of the one and the dependance of the other is greater or less, absolute or limited. And consequently as man depends absolutely upon his maker for every thing, it is necessary that he should in all points conform to his maker's will.[20]

That "will" to which Blackstone refers is the will of God. For Blackstone, God is the only possible source of an absolute moral code:

CONSIDERING the creator only as a being of infinite power, he was able unquestionably to have prescribed whatever laws he pleased to his creature, man. . . . But as he is also a being of infinite wisdom, he has laid down only such laws as were founded in those relations of justice, that existed in the nature of things antecedent to any positive precept. These are the eternal, immutable laws of good and evil, to which the creator himself in all his dispensations conforms; and which he has enabled human reason to discover, so far as they are necessary for the conduct of human actions.[21]

These "eternal, immutable laws of good and evil" are summarized in the Decalogue, and the philosophical foundation upon which our civilization was built acknowledged this truth without hesitation. Today, Blackstone's words sound like the ravings of a madman. However, it is not Blackstone, but modern men in their quest for moral freedom who have actually gone mad.

The Truth We Must Define and Defend

One problem with this approach is, therefore, no limit to where it could lead, what happens if or when the consensus wants to lower or eliminate

CHAPTER 8

Is It Fair to Use the Bible?

A t the time of this writing, I have been preaching and teaching on these issues for more than two decades. At times, I find myself engaged in discussions or debates in which my interlocutors always say something like, "You believe the Bible, and that's fine for you, but you can't force your beliefs on others." Whenever I ask them what I am supposed to use if not the Bible, they always say democratic consensus and protecting the rights of minorities.

Democratic consensus is the belief that we should decide what is or is not acceptable in the realm of human sexuality based on public opinion—just take a vote. If most people want same-sex marriage, puberty blockers for kids, Drag Queen Story Hour in schools, biological males in women's prisons, or biological male athletes competing in women's sports, then we should have those things.

One problem with this approach is that it has no moral compass and, therefore, no limit to where it could lead. What happens if or when the consensus wants to lower or eliminate the age of consent to allow sex between adults and children? What do we do when non-custodial parents want to transition their seven-year-old to another gender? What about incest and bestiality? Where does it end? And again, for those who say "Nobody in their right mind would approve of those things," I remind you, that's exactly what we said about same-sex marriage and having men in women's bathrooms, prisons, and sports fifty years ago.

The other problem with this approach is that it shifts over time. What "democratic consensus" approves of today could be abhorrent soon. For example, there was a time when the democratic consensus approved of chattel slavery. Are we ready to say that was a good moral choice? Should we reinstate it if public consensus changes again? How about anti-miscegenation laws? Is anyone up for taking away women's right to vote? Democratic consensus doesn't pass the common-sense test.

The "protected minority" approach argues that sexual minorities (like other minorities) should not have their options dictated by the whims of the majority. In fact, this is the crux of the "gay is the new black" argument. However, this approach also suffers from a fatal flaw: What, exactly, constitutes a "protected minority"?

People can enjoy minority status for any number of reasons, but let's just go back to the list that the Left has already presented as potential candidates. Members of the North American Man-Boy Love Association (whose motto is "Eight Is Too Late") are sexual minorities. So are those who commit incest and bestiality. I am not just grasping at extremes, but making a point that should be obvious: If we decide what we will or will not condone in the realm of human sexuality without the benefit of a set standard, there is no limit to the levels of debauchery and chaos into which we will sink.

A Better Way

A third approach, the one I'm proposing, is that we rely on the same standard to which we have held since our nation's founding: the Bible. Before you throw down this book and run to social media accusing me of promoting theocracy, allow me to offer examples and an explanation.

Two examples place my position in the heart of the mainstream. The first is the civil rights movement. Many of its leaders, including Dr. King, were pastors who frequently used Scripture to appeal for their rights, on the assumption that America was founded on the very biblical principles to which they were appealing.

So why should we use the Bible as our standard for sexuality? There are three main reasons.

First, marriage is the purview of neither the state nor religion, because it predates both. What Genesis tells us about the first marriage is not an account of a religious rite, but a creation ordinance. Both religion and civil government merely acknowledge this ordinance. Neither has the right to redefine it.

Second, the Bible is the foundation upon which Western civilization is built. (If you don't believe me, just ask anybody who wants to condemn the West for slavery.) Whatever marriage has been in the West, the Bible laid the framework. Even those who disagree with the biblical-traditional model of marriage use other biblical arguments (i.e., "Jesus never talked about homosexuality," "we should support loving relationships because God is love," etc.). As such, it is foolish to attempt to define marriage without referencing the Bible.

Third, the Bible is not only our shared foundation, but our shared standard. Alan Bloom's excellent work, *The Closing of the American Mind*, is quite informative here. He writes:

> In the United States, practically speaking, the Bible was the only common culture, one that united the simple and the sophisticated, rich and poor, young and old. . . . [It provides] the very model for a vision of the order of the whole of things, as well as the key to the rest of Western art, the greatest works of which were in one way or another responsive to the Bible—provided access to the seriousness of books.[1]

For too long, Christians have swallowed the poison pill of trying to make secular arguments for our theological convictions. All arguments about ultimate truth are, in effect, religious arguments. The devout secularist is not free of theological presuppositions. He is as dogmatic as I am. The difference is that he does not acknowledge his presuppositions. Instead, he pretends to be a dispassionate seeker of truth. That, dear reader, is a lie! We are all making religious arguments, and I refuse to set mine aside. To do so would be intellectual suicide. Moreover, as I will demonstrate below, the secular progressives are more than happy to apply biblical arguments when it suits them, and have made heroes of others who do so.

Unfortunately, some of the hardest people to convince of the rightness of arguing from biblical authority are Christians. With that in mind, allow me a brief excursus.

COVID-19, the Church, and the Civil Magistrate

The worldwide lockdowns and mask mandates of 2020–21 led to myriad discussions and debates about the authority of the civil government in relation to the other God-ordained spheres (self-government, family government, and church government). The vast majority of Christians around the world fell on the extreme end of the spectrum that saw civil government as virtually absolute. Few chose to challenge that assumption, and those who did faced the ire not only of the civil government, but of their fellow believers as well.

Why? Because of Romans 13, which states:

> Let every person be subject to the governing authorities. For there is no authority except from God, and those that exist have been instituted by God. Therefore whoever resists the authorities resists what God has appointed, and those who resist will incur judgment. For rulers are not a terror to good conduct, but to bad. Would you have no fear of the one who is in authority? Then do what is good, and you will receive his approval, for he is God's servant for your good. But if you do wrong, be afraid, for he does not bear the sword in vain. For he is the servant of God, an avenger who carries out God's wrath on the wrongdoer. Therefore one must be in subjection, not only to avoid God's wrath but also for the sake of conscience. (Romans 13:1–5)

Perhaps the most famous (or infamous) resisters among evangelical Christians were James Coates in Canada and John MacArthur in America—both of whom I've served with. In

February 2021, Coates broke provincial law by allowing his congregation at GraceLife Church of Edmonton to gather for worship in person—without masks or requiring physical distancing, and disregarding the limit on 15 percent of the building capacity.[2] As a result, he spent a month in jail. Coates is a humble, godly man, full of conviction, who does not believe that Romans 13 gives the civil magistrate the right to command what God forbids—or to forbid what God commands.

MacArthur has been the pastor of Grace Community Church in Sun Valley, California, for over fifty years and is one of the most well-known preachers in the world. In 2020, he became known not for his preaching, but for his defiance of California's strict COVID-19 regulations when he sued Governor Gavin Newsom and other state, county, and city officials for violating the church's First Amendment rights through its draconian measures to limit in-person church activity—including singing!—while allowing bars and liquor stores to stay open as "essential businesses."[3] County officials then countersued the church to force it to comply.

But in September 2021, the case came to an abrupt end when the Los Angeles County Board of Supervisors—and then the state government—settled with Grace Community Church, paying $400,000 apiece to do so.[4]

Few passages of Scripture have been bandied about in the past few years as much as Romans 13. Both those who opposed and those who complied with COVID restrictions pointed to this chapter as the grounds for their decision.

What does all this have to do with same-sex "marriage" or sexual minorities? Because if you think the government will not try to force all churches to perform and recognize same-sex marriage in the same way they forced COVID restrictions on us, you are naïve. The only place we can go from here is a full-frontal assault on the Church and religious freedom. If being homosexual, or trans, or any other letter on the spectrum, is the moral equivalent of being black, then the Church has no more right to discriminate against those behaviors than it does to discriminate against multiethnic people. And if same-sex marriage has been the gate through which other "sexual minorities" are to gain public acceptance, then we ain't seen nothin' yet. When that day comes, we had better be settled on our understanding of Romans 13 *and* our willingness to stand firm in our convictions despite the costs.

With that in mind, let's examine the text itself.

We Must Be Subject to Governing Authorities

Paul clearly calls Christians to submit to civil authority. There is no question about that. In fact, the enemies of Christ and Christianity love to remind us of this when political decisions don't go our way. If our side advances, they demonize Christianity. If our side is defeated, they quickly point to the reality that "elections have consequences," "the people have spoken," and that our faith calls us to submit to authority. Those things are all true.

However, does this mean that Paul was saying we must obey even when civil authorities come into direct conflict with God's revealed will? Of course not![5] Rather, it raises questions like,

1. What does it mean to "be subject" to authority?
2. Are there limits to that subjection?

3. What constitutes a "governing authority" in a given setting?
4. What is the theological basis for our subjection to said authority?

All Authority Comes from God

Paul gives us clear answers to those questions.

> For there is no authority except from God, and those that exist have been instituted by God. (Romans 13:1)

Having established the fact that we must be subject to governing authorities, we now turn to the why. On what basis must we be subject? John Calvin put it quite simply: "The reason why we ought to be subject to magistrates is because they are constituted by God's ordination."[6] Robert Mounce builds on this sentiment, writing,

> there is no authority apart from that which God has established. He alone is the sole source of authority, and it has pleased him to delegate authority to those in charge of the public well-being.[7]

Or as Charles Simeon put it,

> God is the Governor of all the earth: and, as all power is derived from him, so all power is delegated by him; the possessor of it being his representative and vicegerent.[8] . . . Whatever shape the different governments assumed, monarchical, aristocratical, or democratical [sic],

still the power was God's, in whomsoever it was vested: and, as his representatives, they possessed and exercised a portion of his authority.[9]

Put simply, we obey civil authority because it, like all authority, comes from God.

The inevitable question is, "Are there limits?" The answer is yes. No man can command what God forbids or forbid what God commands. If they do, we have two apostles as our examples of the appropriate Christian response. When commanded by the authorities to stop preaching and teaching in the name of Jesus,

> Peter and John answered them, "Whether it is right in the sight of God to listen to you rather than to God, you must judge, for we cannot but speak of what we have seen and heard." (Acts 4:19–20)

When, Why, and How Do We Defy Governing Authorities?

Being subject to governing authority can be viewed in two ways: absolute or limited. If it is absolute, then we must literally do whatever the authorities say whenever they say to do it. This, of course, is untenable for a couple of reasons. As we will see, several biblical figures contradict such a reading (i.e., Moses, Daniel, Peter, etc.). Second, we have historical precedents like the abolitionist movement, the civil rights movement, and pro-life movement, to name a few, that are almost universally understood to be legitimate Christian protests in defiance of illegitimate exercises of authority. Moreover, during the Nuremberg trials, no one believed the German officers who said, "We're not guilty, because the governing authorities told us to torture and exterminate Jews." We all know that some orders are immoral on their face and should be defied. For these reasons, it is obvious that the authority of the civil magistrate is not absolute, but limited.

So what limits the civil magistrate's authority? What made slavery, Jim Crow laws, and abortion untenable? What made Nazi orders to exterminate Jews reprehensible? The answer to these questions is twofold. First, the magistrate is limited by the law of the land. This is why we have laws, constitutions, courts, and law enforcement. Granted, these things are all flawed. They are *proximate* forms of justice. There has to be something more—something higher.

But there is something higher: the Law of God. That is what limits the civil magistrate's authority. This is not just my idea; it is the idea upon which the United States of America was established. Recall the words of the Declaration of Independence:

> When in the Course of human events, it becomes necessary for one people to dissolve the political bands which have connected them with another, and to assume among the powers of the earth, the separate and equal station to which the Laws of Nature and of Nature's God entitle them, a decent respect to the opinions of mankind requires that they should declare the causes which impel them to the separation.[10]

Two things are clear here: 1) The Founding Fathers acknowledged and respected the ultimate source of governing authority.

Note the appeal to "the Laws of Nature and of Nature's God. 2) There is also an acknowledgment of and respect for the penultimate or proximate source of governing authority—namely, "the political bonds which" connect men (i.e., constitutions, laws, etc.), and "the consent of the governed."

This is not a cherry-picked example. The next section of the Declaration reiterates the same two principles:

> We hold these truths to be self-evident, that all men are created equal, that they are endowed by their Creator with certain unalienable Rights, that among these are Life, Liberty and the pursuit of Happiness. That to secure these rights, Governments are instituted among Men, deriving their just powers from the consent of the governed, That whenever any Form of Government becomes destructive of these ends, it is the Right of the People to alter or to abolish it, and to institute new Government, laying its foundation on such principles and organizing its powers in such form, as to them shall seem most likely to effect their Safety and Happiness.[11]

Again, note the acknowledgment of God as the ultimate source of governing authority. And again we see that the laws men make are understood to be subject to the aforementioned Law of God. Finally, we see that when the laws men make usurp the Law of God, men ought to form new governments.

Of course, those who oppose this view will argue that the Declaration lacks moral authority because at the time it was written, some men were slaves and women did not have the right to vote. To which I respond: Yes! And both issues were confronted and rectified *because* of the truth of the aforementioned principles. Abolition and the civil rights movement did not argue for equality based on notions alien to the Constitution and Declaration. On the contrary, they referenced both documents extensively! More importantly, far from being secular movements that argued in the abstract, both pointed to the Law of God that undergirds the Declaration and Constitution as the source of the moral authority in their arguments.

Nowhere is this more evident than in what is arguably the most popular, if not most important, speech in American history, Martin Luther King Jr.'s "I Have a Dream." We see it in the most familiar lines of the speech:

> I still have a dream. It is a dream deeply rooted in the American dream. I have a dream that one day this nation will rise up and live out the true meaning of its creed. *We hold these truths to be self-evident that all men are created equal.*[12]

But we also see it in the lesser known but equally important introduction of the speech, where King specifically references the Constitution and Declaration as the source of his argument:

> In a sense we have come to our Nation's Capital to cash a check. When the architects of our great republic wrote the magnificent words of the Constitution and the Declaration of Independence, they were signing a promissory note to which every American was to fall heir . . . This note was a promise that all men, yes, black men as well as white men,

would be guaranteed the inalienable rights of life, liberty, and the pursuit of happiness.[13]

While King was certainly a flawed man with whose theology and morality I have many issues, the point is that there is a long and well-documented history of the fundamental principles I am espousing. We have all agreed for a long time that governing authority is limited. We have also agreed (recent departures notwithstanding) that there is a Law higher than the magistrate's, and it is to that law he must be held. This is why "We must obey God rather than men" (Acts 5:29).

Another important matter to settle is the role of governing authorities.

The Righteous Role of the Civil Government: Reward Good, Punish Evil

Most of the talk about Romans 13 centers on Christians' duty to the civil magistrate. There is another side to that coin that is rarely discussed but which is vitally important.

> For rulers are not a terror to good conduct, but to bad. Would you have no fear of the one who is in authority? Then do what is good, and you will receive his approval, for he is God's servant for your good. But if you do wrong, be afraid, for he does not bear the sword in vain. For he is the servant of God, an avenger who carries out God's wrath on the wrongdoer. Therefore one must be in subjection, not only to avoid God's wrath but also for the sake of conscience. (Romans 13:3–5)

Paul makes it clear that the "rulers" about whom he speaks are those who approve of good conduct and are a terror to bad conduct. These thoughts are not his alone. King Solomon wrote:

A king who sits on the throne of judgment winnows all evil with his eyes. (Proverbs 20:8)

A wise king winnows the wicked and drives the wheel over them. (Proverbs 20:26)

John Calvin's comments also are instructive:

Magistrates may hence learn what their vocation is, for they are not to rule for their own interest, but for the public good; nor are they endued with unbridled power, but what is restricted to the wellbeing of their subjects; in short, they are responsible to God and to men in the exercise of their power.[14]

Douglas Moo echoes this sentiment in his commentary on Romans, writing, "governmental authorities are established by God to serve his purposes of rewarding good and punishing evil."[15] Quotes to this effect are myriad among Christian scholars both ancient and modern.

In reading Romans 13:2, it is important to note that Paul is addressing the ruler who is performing his duty under God. It is only in that context that resisting his rule equals "resisting the divine ordinance." Clearly, Paul is not "establishing a universally valid principle that opposing the authority and disobeying a command issued by a civil magistrate is always wrong." That cannot be the case since God's Law is always the ultimate authority.

Paul's Example

Two examples in Scripture make it clear the Apostle Paul was not advocating unlimited subjection to governing authority: Acts 16 and Acts 22.

In Acts 16, Paul and Silas had been arrested and put in jail in Philippi. As they prayed at midnight, there was an earthquake. Their chains fell off and their doors were opened. Then, in one of the most dramatic scenes in the New Testament, we read:

> When the jailer woke and saw that the prison doors were open, he drew his sword and was about to kill himself, supposing that the prisoners had escaped. But Paul cried with a loud voice, "Do not harm yourself, for we are all here." And the jailer called for lights and rushed in, and trembling with fear he fell down before Paul and Silas. Then he brought them out and said, "Sirs, what must I do to be saved?" And they said, "Believe in the Lord Jesus, and you will be saved, you and your household." (Acts 16:27–31)

A jailer who lost his prisoners was subject to capital punishment. Hence, the guard was about to do "the honorable thing" and kill himself. However, his prisoners had not left. They had more pressing business, like preaching the Gospel to the jailer, who eventually came to repentance and faith—along with his entire household! But that's not the end of the story:

> But when it was day, the magistrates sent the police, saying, "Let those men go." And the jailer reported these words to Paul, saying, "The magistrates have sent to let you go. Therefore come out now and go in peace." (Acts 16:35–36)

If Paul was advocating for unquestioning, unlimited submission to governing authority, or if he believed that the magistrate himself was the authority (and not the Law of God to which the magistrate is accountable), the scene would end here with Paul obediently leaving Philippi. However, it does not:

> But Paul said to them, "They have beaten us publicly, uncondemned, men who are Roman citizens, and have thrown us into prison; and do they now throw us out secretly? No! Let them come themselves and take us out." The police reported these words to the magistrates, and they were afraid when they heard that they were Roman citizens. So they came and apologized to them. And they took them out and asked them to leave the city. (Acts 16:37–39)

Note that Paul appeals to the authority above the local magistrate: As a Roman citizen, he appealed to the law of the Roman Empire. He knew his rights and he demanded them, regardless of the order given by the magistrate. Do you hear the echoes of civil rights leaders defying the laws of the Jim Crow South and appealing to higher authority?

In Acts 22, Paul was about to be flogged.

> But when they had stretched him out for the whips, Paul said to the centurion who was standing by, "Is it lawful for you to flog a man who is a Roman citizen and uncondemned?" (Acts 22:25)

Again, rather than just doing what he was told, he appealed to the law. As a result,

> those who were about to examine him withdrew from him immediately, and the tribune also was afraid, for he realized that Paul was a Roman citizen and that he had bound him. (Acts 22:29)

Clearly, the Apostle Paul had no intention of teaching absolute obedience to human authority. There is a higher authority to whom both we and our human authorities must answer.

Doctrine of the Lesser Magistrate

At the end of WWII, the world was astonished to discover the atrocities of the Nazi regime—the medical experimentation, the starvation, the torture, the forced labor, the gas chambers. Many wondered how men could have done that to their fellow human beings. Few were moved by the common refrain, "We were just following orders." We knew then, as we know now, that some orders should not be followed. Somewhere in the chain of command, someone has to be willing to appeal to a higher authority. In Christian theology, this is sometimes referred to as the doctrine of the lesser magistrate.

This, writes Matthew Trewhella,

> declares that when the superior or higher civil authority makes unjust/immoral laws or decrees, the lesser or lower ranking civil authority has both a right and duty to refuse obedience to that superior authority.[16]

In some cases, "the lesser authorities even have the right and obligation to actively resist the superior authority."[17] A classic example of this is when Daniel refused to obey King Darius's decree not to pray for thirty days. Daniel was acting as a lesser magistrate when he defied the king. Another is when colonial leaders decided to defy King George's usurious edicts by writing the Declaration of Independence.

Nor is this concept foreign to the American framework. Trewhella notes that

> The teaching by Christian men about the lesser magistrate, God's sovereignty, covenant, the nature of man, and church government shaped the views of Western Civilization that birthed constitutional governments.[18]

This is a universally accepted principle of American jurisprudence—and we saw it in action when marriage licenses were issued to same-sex couples in 2004. San Francisco mayor Gavin Newsom, who had only been in office twelve days, was bothered by the fact that President George W. Bush had announced that he wanted to amend the U.S. Constitution to protect the biblical definition of marriage. Newsom was "disgusted and outraged,"[19] so he proceeded to engage in an act of interposition as a lesser magistrate by issuing marriage licenses to same-sex couples. And he was seen as a hero in the LGBTQ community for doing so. They did not have a problem with his alleged Catholicism, his heterosexuality, or his whiteness. Nor did they have a problem with him imposing his own morality by fiat. They saw him doing what they wanted him to do. He wasn't acting as a lesser magistrate for a higher moral purpose; he was personally out-raged. That was his motivation.

As I have said before, at the end of the day, all republics are religious in nature, and all laws are fundamentally moral. The issue in the West is that republics founded upon Christian foundations have decided that they are ashamed of their heritage, and vocal minorities are taking advantage of that shame—not to remove religion altogether, but to impose their woke, pagan, neo-Marxist religion under the guise of secular neutrality. Unfortunately, many of us have not only been gullible enough to believe their deception, but have also decided that their fundamental premise that Christianity has no place in the public square is correct. We continue to try to use secular arguments to convince secularists that their secularism is wrong. We fail to recognize that making arguments that ignore Scripture is conceding before we start.

The Bible gave birth to Western civilization. It has sustained us since the beginning. It is our only hope of survival in generations to come. It is our only bulwark against moral decay, and the only source of true tolerance. Without it, we either will devolve into warring factions of religious enclaves pretending that there is such a thing as secular democracy—or we can repent, go back to our foundations, and seek to rebuild our sexual morality according to a higher law.

CHAPTER 9

What Happens When
We Buy the Lie?

We cannot contradict Scripture, change thousands of years of tradition, subvert the English language, and deny fundamental reality without paying a heavy price. To quote the title of one of my favorite R. C. Sproul books, "Ideas have consequences." And when it comes to the sexual identity movement, the idea with the greatest and farthest-reaching consequences has been the legalization of same-sex marriage.

The LGBTQIA2S+ lobby would have us believe that a victory for their cause was a victory for society as a whole. After all, we are the land of the free and the home of the tolerant. However, gay marriage greased the slope that our nation is now sliding down with increasing speed—and many more deleterious things await us at the bottom.

The End of Marriage

The most obvious consequence attending the acceptance of same sex marriage was the end to marriage as we knew it. In fact, this is the most obvious and indisputable consequence, since the entire discussion centered around redefining it. Marriage is the most fundamental institution in the history of mankind; defining it is a bit like defining what it means to be human. Humans have always been fundamentally different from all the other animals on the planet, and therefore needed no definition. But since *Obergefell*, all that has changed with marriage—and could change again to include still other types of arrangements. We'll get into that in a moment, but first, let's look at some of the subtle but vital changes that have already taken place.

One clue is the change in our language. You may have noticed the increasingly common use of the term "partner" in place of "husband" or "wife." There are several reasons for this: It eliminates the favored status of marriage. It is an insult, reducing a husband or wife to the same status as a doubles partner in tennis, a lab partner in science class, or a business partner in the corporate world. When we introduce someone as "my wife" (or "my husband"), we confer status on that relationship that can never be matched by any other kind.

Second, "partner" eliminates the awkwardness of referring to people in same-sex unions as "wife and wife" or "husband and husband." You can't be a husband without a wife (or a wife without a husband). We all know this, no matter how many times we are told otherwise. When a woman says, "This is my wife," alarms go off in our brains. Unfortunately, we are being conditioned to either ignore those alarms, or worse, to instantly accuse and condemn ourselves for our intolerance and backward thinking—and then to congratulate that person on their marriage.

A third reason for switching to the term "partner" is the rise in cohabitation, which has accompanied the decline in marriage. People who are living together without the benefit of marriage (once referred to as "shacking up" or having a "common-law marriage") cannot only avoid stigma, but are also instantly elevated to the same cultural status of married people. Another side effect of this is that even the terms "boyfriend" and "girlfriend" seem to be used less often, which could pave the way for greater acceptance of some of the weirder "orientations" we've touched on in this book. With that one word, it seems *all* the boundary lines are being erased.

Redefining marriage opened a door that may be impossible to close. Since we've accepted this in the name of accommodating "sexual minorities," how will we say no to incest, polygamy, or polyamory?

Polygamy

Those who chafe at the idea of linking same-sex marriage with incest, polygamy, polyamory, and other aberrant lifestyles are naïve at best. But even the most casual observer has to recognize the slippery slope inherent in their argument. Stanley Kurtz pointed this out twenty years ago in *The Weekly Standard*, writing:

When Tom Green was put on trial in Utah for polygamy in 2001, it played like a dress rehearsal for the coming movement to legalize polygamy. True, Green was convicted for violating what he called Utah's "don't ask, don't tell" policy on polygamy. Pointedly refusing to "hide in the closet," he touted polygamy on the Sally Jessy Raphael, Queen Latifah, Geraldo Rivera, and Jerry Springer shows, and on *Dateline NBC* and *48 Hours*. . . . It brought out a surprising number of mainstream defenses of polygamy. And most of the defenders went to bat for polygamy *by drawing direct comparisons to gay marriage*.[1] (emphasis mine)

While gay marriage advocates still deflect this with statements like, "Nobody's talking about polygamy," the truth is quite different. *Big Love*, a show that aired on HBO from 2006 to 2011 and was produced by Tom Hanks, was about a polygamist "family" in Utah. And polygamists were very pleased with it. As one news source reported, "despite the show's flaws, [polygamist] women called *Big Love* a cultural benchmark, one with the potential to cast a warmer light on their lives."[2] And this was not some backwoods Utah newspaper; it was the *New York Times*. (For those paying attention, this is called *desensitizing*.)

Polygamists' cries for acceptance sound eerily similar to those heard previously in the same-sex marriage movement. A widow who had shared her husband with his other wives for thirty-three years praised *Big Love* by saying:

> "It's a more realistic view of a polygamous family that lives out in society than people have known. . . . It can be seen as a *viable alternative lifestyle between consenting adults*."[3] (emphasis mine)

The idea that "alternative lifestyles" should be accepted and that "consenting adults" should be able not only to determine their own sexual practices but have them recognized and sanctioned by the state is far from a new concept. The Iowa Supreme Court used exactly that to legalize same-sex marriage in 2009.

> Therefore, with respect to the subject and purposes of Iowa's marriage laws, we find that the plaintiffs are similarly situated compared to heterosexual persons. Plaintiffs *are in committed and loving relationships, many raising families, just like heterosexual couples.*[4] (emphasis mine)

Polyamory

If the only thing required for the state to recognize a union is a "committed and loving relationship" between people "raising families just like [heterosexual/monogamous] couples," then we need to brace ourselves for more stories like that of Ari, Gwendolyn, and Brenifer, a nonbinary throuple in Florida raising two genderless children.[5] Polygamy may be the most obvious next step in the battle over marriage, but polyamory will come after that. While polygamy usually involves marriage between one man and many women, polyamory could involve any number and configuration of men and women. One definition in the "peer-reviewed" *Electronic Journal of Human Sexuality* offered a definition I simply could not pass up:

> Polyamory has been defined as the philosophy and practice of loving more than one person at a time with honesty and integrity. Synonyms for polyamory are *responsible, ethical, and intentional, non-monogamy.* Because those descriptions are somewhat clumsy, the term Polyamory was coined in the late 80's by a pagan Priestess, Morning

Glory Zell, and defines a range of different lifestyle alternatives. In most cases, but not all, this involves some sexual or at least intensely intimate sensual behavior.[6] (emphasis mine)

Thus, if your "non-monogamy" is irresponsible, unethical, or unintentional, it doesn't qualify as polyamory. (If you are wondering, *How can non-monogamy be ethical?*, join the club!)

Though it may be difficult for some to grasp, this is not a joke. In fact, some lawyers have been thinking, writing, arguing, and moving in this direction for quite some time. In 2003, University of Chicago Law School professor Elizabeth Emens offered a glimpse of the future when she wrote:

[T]he practice of polyamory as "ethical nonmonogamy" bears serious consideration at a moment when the terms and conditions of intimate relationships are such a focus of discussion. Polyamory is a lifestyle embraced by a minority of individuals, who exhibit a wide variety of relationship models and who articulate an ethical vision that I understand to encompass five main principles: self-knowledge, radical honesty, consent, self-possession, and privileging love and sex over jealousy. Contrary to the common view of multi-party relationships as either oppressive or sexual free-for-alls, at least some set of individuals—polyamorists, or "polys" for short—seems to be practicing nonmonogamy as part of an ethical practice that shares some of its aspirations with more mainstream models of intimate relationships.[7]

Note that Emens is writing about an actual movement. Polyamory is a growing phenomenon. She points to "Loving More" as an example of the organized voice of the movement, writing,

> No studies or surveys estimate the number of people cur-
> rently engaged in polyamory, but the national organiza-
> tion Loving More reports a rate of 1,000 hits per day
> on its website and a circulation of 10,000 readers for its
> eponymous magazine.[8]

Remember, that was published in 2004. There has certainly been an uptick in traffic and participation since then.

In 2006, the international "gay rights" group Beyond Same-Sex Marriage gave us a look behind the scenes by releasing a statement (complete with high-profile signatories) outlining its beliefs.

> The struggle for same-sex marriage rights is only one part
> of a larger effort to strengthen the security and stability of
> diverse households and families. LGBT communities have
> ample reason to recognize that families and relationships
> *know no borders and will never slot narrowly into a single
> existing template.* . . . To have our government define as
> "legitimate families" only those households with couples
> in conjugal relationships does a tremendous disservice to
> the many other ways in which people actually construct
> their families, kinship networks, households, and relation-
> ships. For example, who among us seriously will argue
> that the following kinds of households are less socially,
> economically, and spiritually worthy?[9] (emphasis mine)

According to the statement, the types of relationships on which the signatories wanted to confer the benefits of marriage included:

- Senior citizens living together, serving as each other's caregivers, partners, and/or constructed families
- Adult children living with and caring for their parents
- Grandparents and other family members raising their children's (and/or a relative's) children
- Committed, loving households in which there is more than one conjugal partner
- Blended families
- Single-parent households
- Extended families (especially in particular immigrant populations) living under one roof, whose members care for one another
- Queer couples who decide to jointly create and raise a child with another queer person or couple, in two households
- Close friends and siblings who live together in long-term, committed, nonconjugal relationships, serving as each other's primary support and caregivers
- Caregiving and partnership relationships that have been developed to provide support systems to those living with HIV/AIDS

In other words, if anyone can be married, then everyone can be married. Because marriage just isn't special at all.

But wait: There's more.

Pedophilia

Sexual minority advocates have always groaned about including pedophilia in the discussion. However, despite those moans and groans, the issue must be addressed. There are simply too many parallels (and touchstones) with the gay-rights movement to ignore the fact that pedophilia has worked its way out of society's forbidden closet to a place that is visible, if not unavoidable. And the trajectory has been a virtual mirror image of the one that led to the acceptance of same-sex marriage.

In 1973, the American Psychiatric Association reclassified homosexuality in the Diagnostic and Statistical Manual (DSM) from a "disorder" to a "sexual orientation disturbance," paving the way for its greater public acceptance.[10] In 2005, the APA responded similarly to pedophilia activists, which[11] led some to "express concern that this would pave the way for reduced criminal culpability[12] for raping children."[13] Today the APA distinguishes between Pedophilic Disorder and a pedophilic sexual orientation. Pedophilic Disorder is accompanied by feelings of guilt and shame, but the orientation "involves the absence of anxiety, shame, or guilt at being sexually attracted to children."[14] In other words, unless one's desire for sex with children causes shame, anxiety, or guilt, there isn't a problem, and we should regard pedophiles in exactly the same way as everyone else on the LGBTQIA2S+ spectrum.

In addition to reclassification, Pedophilic Disorder, like homosexuality, has gone through a favorable change in terminology. In November 2022, Old Dominion sociology and criminology professor Allyn Walker caused a stir when he asserted that there is a "need to destigmatize pedophiles by redefining them as 'minor-attracted persons.'"[15] A month later, Libs of

TikTok shared a video in which State University of New York professor Stephen Kershnar admitted that he disagrees with the "very standard, very widely held view that there's something deeply wrong about [sex between an adult male and a twelve-year-old girl]." Kershnar said, "It's not obvious to me that it is in fact wrong." In another video, Kershnar cited "metastudies" suggesting that that there's nothing harmful to underage males about sex with adult men; or "if it is harmful, we can't decide whether the harm is due to the sex itself or the fact that society goes berserk over it."[16]

Remember what we discussed previously about the writings of queer theorists Gayle Rubin and Hannah Dyer? Queer theory is neither a stranger to nor an opponent of pedophilia. As far back as 1977, activists including Michel Foucault and Simone de Beauvoir were petitioning the French government to lower the age of consent to thirteen.[17] Before dying of AIDS at the age of fifty-seven, Foucault—who is revered by those advocating for changing terminology to "minor-attracted persons"—was living in Tunisia, reportedly paying to have sex with eight-year-old boys.[18]

The End of Women

Today, the tip of the spear in the "sexual minority" arena is the trans movement. Gone are the days of arguing over what consenting men and women should be allowed to do in the privacy of their bedrooms (and have the state recognize as legitimate). Now, we are arguing over the very definition of the words "man" and "woman." Unfortunately, the result of that argument is catastrophic for women.

Much of the recent focus has been directed to erasing women from the podiums and record books of sports. Whether it's cycling, track and field, weightlifting, swimming, MMA, or basketball, we have seen biological males win championships and set records by competing with women.

However, sports is not the only arena where women are being erased. Now they're even losing to men in beauty pageants! In June 2021, twenty-seven-year-old biological male Kataluna Enriquez, who had only begun competing in cisgender pageants a year earlier, was crowned Miss Nevada USA.[19] In November 2022, Brian (pronounced Bree-ann) Nguyen won New Hampshire's Miss Derry pageant, becoming the first transgender competitor to win a local competition in the Miss America Organization.[20] And in March 2023, twenty-five-year-old Monroe Lace became the first biological male to win the Miss San Francisco beauty queen pageant in its ninety-nine-year history. (He said his goal is to be a "role model for young children.")[21]

Now, women are even being erased from the English language. Since 2020, we have seen even our federal elected officials using terms like "menstruating people," "birthing people," or "pregnant people" instead of "women." There have also been debates over using the term "mother" because we are now being told that men who "identify" as women can do all these things too, and we don't want to offend anyone![22]

Despite what radical feminists claim, Western civilization has done more to protect and advance the rights of women than any other culture in history, and America has been exceptional in that regard—until now, when we are actively seeking to erase their uniqueness from our society by insulting them in these ways.

The End of Tolerance

"Gay marriage was the first great triumph of cancel culture," wrote Matthew Schmitz in the April 2023 edition of *First Things*. Schmitz makes a compelling argument that, starting with the battle over California's Prop 8 in 2008, the fight for normalizing same-sex marriage gave rise to new levels of intolerance, and *Obergefell* only made things worse.

> Legal protection of gay rights has entailed the penalization of traditional views of marriage. . . . Any employer or employee who expresses opposition to homosexuality in stark or unsubtle terms can be regarded as creating a hostile work environment or engaging in hate speech.[23]

This is the fruit of the sexual-minority revolution. We have all seen the way that "high-profile opponents of same-sex marriage were silenced, fired, or forced out of important institutions" over the last decade.[24] Schmitz's list is not exhaustive, but it is very telling:

- In order to continue his work defending the federal law defining marriage and the union of one man and one woman, former U.S. solicitor general Paul Clement was compelled to leave his law firm in 2011 after the Human Rights Campaign pressured the firm to drop the case.
- In 2015, Atlanta fire chief Kelvin Cochran was fired after writing a book saying heterosexuality is God's design for mankind.
- In 2023, Georgia police officer Jacob Kersey was placed on leave after stating on Facebook: "God designed

marriage. Marriage refers to Christ and the church. That's why there is no such thing as homosexual marriage."[25]

True tolerance is a thing of the past. The success of the "gay is the new black" mantra has led to the inevitable conclusion that anyone who opposes same-sex marriage—and by extension, any part of the ever-expanding acronym—has crossed a line and must be numbered among those we must not tolerate, in the name of tolerance.

The End of Reason

Anyone who has ever studied logic cannot help but cringe in the face of the current sexual-minority debate. The abuse of reason commonly displayed in this arena does not bode well for the future. No longer do people rely on cogent, winsome, well-thought-out arguments to gain political ground; the winning strategy now is demonizing your opponent, relying on slogans and soundbites regardless of the facts, and always remembering that emotion trumps reason. One of the key ways we see that being done is through question-begging logic.

Anyone who has watched the news lately has heard a reporter say, "That begs the question . . ." Unfortunately, the way this phrase is used in everyday speech usually bears very little resemblance to its actual meaning. When most people say something "begs the question," what they actually mean is that it "raises" the question—which is not the same.

The phrase "begging the question," or "petitio principii" in Latin, refers to the "question" in a formal debate—that is, the issue being debated. In such a debate, one side may ask the other side to concede certain points in order to speed up the proceedings. To "beg" the question is to ask that the very point at issue be conceded, which is of course illegitimate.[26]

To put it plainly, an argument begs the question when it assumes any controversial point not conceded by the other side.[27] Same-sex marriage advocates beg the question consistently in at least three ways.

One is when they treat homosexual behavior as morally equivalent to blackness. If we concede this point, we throw logic out the window, demean minorities in general and black people in particular, and lay the foundation for further folly down the line. Doing so, as William F. Buckley used to say, is the equivalent of saying that "the man who pushes an old lady into the path of a hurtling bus is not to be distinguished from the man who pushes an old lady out of the path of a hurtling bus: on the grounds that, after all, in both cases someone is pushing old ladies around."[28]

There is a difference between a man who has a high melanin count and a man who enjoys having sex with other men. Unfortunately, some of the worst perpetrators of this fraud are leading public figures who also happen to be black. Former NAACP chief Julien Bond is a prime example. In 2005, he said:

African Americans . . . were the only Americans who were enslaved for two centuries, but we were far from the only Americans suffering discrimination then and now. Sexual disposition parallels race. I was born this way. I have no choice. I wouldn't change it if I could. Sexuality is unchangeable.[29]

This kind of thinking is not exclusive to the political left. When *GQ* asked former Republican National Committee Chairman Michael Steele if he thought homosexuality was a "choice," Steele replied:

Oh, no. I don't think I've ever really subscribed to that view, that you can turn it on and off like a water tap. Um, you know, I think that there's a whole lot that goes into the makeup of an individual that, uh, you just can't simply say, oh, like, "Tomorrow morning I'm gonna stop being gay." It's like saying, "Tomorrow morning I'm gonna stop being black."[30]

This is a classic case of question-begging logic. Who says homosexuality is as immutable as blackness? When did we concede that point?

Then there's the question-begging logic of allowing any two (or possibly more) people "who love each other" to get married. What about the underaged couple? What about the couple who already happen to be married to other people? What about the brother and sister? What about the forty-year-old mayor and his seventeen-year-old lover?[31] Marriage has never been about "two people who love each other." There has always been more to it than that. In fact, even the statement, "two people who love each other" represents restrictions: By saying that, you restrict the number, you eliminate nonpersons, you require love, and you limit that love to the persons in question. So much for tolerance.

Then there's the question-begging logic of "fundamental" rights. The idea that same-sex marriage is a "fundamental right" is wrong on its face. Sodomy was illegal in all thirteen colonies at the founding of the United States of America. How, then, could same-sex marriage be a "fundamental right"? There has never been such a right; there is no religious, philosophical, or political tradition that recognized such a right prior to the last half-century, and there is no logical ground upon which to argue for such a right without question-begging logic.

In America, we have always "taken away" people's rights when we deemed them to be inconsistent with the greater goods of public safety or morality (for example, requiring a person to be licensed to drive, own a gun, fish, hunt, or use a trademark). Virtually every law we pass takes rights away from someone—but only for good reasons that protect the public good. LGBTQIA2S+ activists are asking us to do so based on emotion, and it is harming our children more than anyone. This is bad for society.

The End of the Rule of Law

All parents embarrass their children at times. I am no different. However, the ways in which I embarrass my children are quite unique. Years ago, I was sitting in my office with my favorite song blaring as I engaged in a little casual reading. Suddenly I felt a presence in the room. I looked over my shoulder to find my nineteen-year-old daughter folding her arms and shaking her head as she rolled her eyes and walked away. A few moments later she came back and said, "Other kids walk in and catch their dad listening to cheesy '80s music and reading hot-rod magazines. I walk in and my dad—the big, imposing former football player—is listening to 'Nessum Dorma' and reading Supreme Court decisions."

I am not a lawyer, nor do I play one on television. I am just an American who takes his citizenship seriously and loves the laws that form the foundation upon which our freedom is built. I am also a homeschooling dad who reads the Constitution with his children each year. Moreover, I'm a guy who tries to read key legal decisions when they are handed down so that I know what is actually happening to my liberties, as opposed to getting the information secondhand from some biased talking head on TV.

As a result, I have been appalled lately as I read some of the most convoluted reasoning imaginable in legal decisions handed down by some of our country's leading jurists. Gone are the days when we actually believed in the "rule of law" above the opinions and feelings of men. In his dissent to *Lawrence v. Texas* in 2003—the case that erased all penalties for consensual sodomy between adults—Justice Antonin Scalia wrote:

> I have never heard of a law that attempted to restrict one's "right to define" certain concepts; and if the passage calls into question the government's power to regulate actions based on one's self-defined "concept of existence, etc.," it *is the passage that ate the rule of law.* . . . State laws against bigamy, same-sex marriage, adult incest, prostitution, masturbation, adultery, fornication, bestiality, and obscenity are likewise sustainable only in light of . . . laws based on moral choices. Every single one of these laws is called into question by today's decision; the Court makes no effort to cabin the scope of its decision to exclude them from its holding.[32] (emphasis mine)

It terrifies me to think how many people are completely unaware that there has been a sea change in the practice of law in America. Gone are the days when lawyers and judges were subject to a sovereign Lawgiver and did their best to uphold that law. Now, those who sit on the bench are deemed sovereign. As a result, our law is increasingly becoming no law at all. Scalia's dissent in *Obergefell* rings true:

> Today's decree says that my Ruler, and the Ruler of 320 million Americans coast to coast, is a majority of the nine lawyers on the Supreme Court. The opinion in these cases is the furthest extension in fact—and the furthest extension one can even imagine—of the Court's claimed power to create "liberties" that the Constitution and its Amendments neglect to mention. This practice of constitutional revision by an unelected committee of nine, always accompanied (as it is today) by extravagant praise of liberty, robs the People of the most important liberty they asserted in the Declaration of Independence and won in the Revolution of 1776: the freedom to govern themselves.[33]

More specifically, it robs the people of self-governance "under God." We are in the midst of a pitched battle for the soul of our nation, including reason and law. To ignore these issues will ultimately lead to tragic consequences—and most of what I have covered in this chapter is already coming to fruition. The only question is, how much farther will it go, and how quickly?

CHAPTER 10

God's Design for Marriage

One of my favorite sayings is, "If you don't know the purpose of a thing, you are destined to abuse it." This is true whether you are talking about a widget or a wife. It is certainly true when we are talking about marriage. If we don't know the purpose of marriage, we are destined to abuse it—and that is precisely what many are doing today in myriad ways. At the heart of our misuse is our insistence that we can define marriage without the Creator's input. We simply do not believe it is appropriate (or necessary) to consult the Bible when it comes to marriage and family.

My insistence on rooting my understanding of marriage and the family in the Scriptures is born of two concurrent desires known as the Great Commandments. First, I desire to honor God and love Him with all my heart, soul, mind, and strength (Matthew 22:37). Therefore, I cannot trade God's design for anything less. Second, I desire to love my neighbor as myself (Matthew 22:39). Doing marriage man's way is dangerous, degrading, and painful. I want better for my fellow man. Following God's design is a sure way to achieve that.

The family is the cornerstone of civilization, and the first institution God created. The family is the first and best department of health, education, and welfare, and the foundation of the family is marriage. Therefore, how we choose to define marriage and the family will inevitably impact how we define and build (or destroy) culture.

Marriage is ultimately designed to glorify God and fulfill His purposes in the world. The three main purposes or marriage are procreation, illustration, and sanctification. In this chapter, I will not only define and explain these purposes, but show how they militate against defining marriage and family in ways that incorporate so-called sexual minorities in creative configurations. Since my purpose in this book is to show that the comparison between sexual minorities and ethnic minorities is illegitimate, I will also show how these purposes do support interracial marriage.

We begin with the most controversial of the three: procreation.

Procreation

Procreation as a central purpose and broader standard for marriage has become more controversial in recent generations, and not just because of the same-sex marriage debate. The widespread availability of contraceptives and abortion ended the era when having sex carried the inherent risk of pregnancy and parenthood. The sexual revolution was in many ways a celebration of sex without responsibility. Naïvely, many also thought it meant the availability of sex without consequence—but there is no such thing.

It's totally fine to be critical of social norms—and in fact, I think we should all be skeptical, to some degree—but it's harmful to replace truth with wishful thinking in the name of a larger political goal. . . . It actually hurts women to behave like men, and vice versa, when it comes to courtship and sex. This is the case regardless of one's political affiliation.[1]

The woman who wrote those words, Debra Soh, would definitely not agree with the assertions I'm making in this book—and that makes her assessment even more striking. Even common-grace observation shows us that man cannot pursue sex without restraint and escape consequences.

This rise in childless sex has also given rise to the idea that marriage centered on procreation is an archaic, misogynistic, patriarchal idea that belongs on the historical trash heap. Moreover, this attitude opens the door for marriage to be reimagined. If marriage is about something more "significant" than procreation, then it is both easy and natural to assume that the male/female distinctive is unnecessary—even oppressive. And that is exactly what "marriage equality" advocates have argued. Unfortunately, many Christians have decided to ignore—or worse, concede—this argument. Neither choice is acceptable.

The argument against procreation as a necessary component of the definition of marriage takes many forms. Most laymen simply argue something like this: "If marriage is about procreation, then you would have to oppose the marriage between people who are too old to procreate." However, we are not arguing that procreation is a *prerequisite* for marriage. We are arguing that procreation is part of the original design of marriage, which gives us, among other things, the male/female distinctive. We recognize that, because of the Fall, not every couple will be able to procreate. However, that does not negate the original design or its implications.

There are more sophisticated versions of this argument. Matthew Vines writes,

> Yes, Adam and Eve were an opposite-sex couple, as was necessary for them to "be fruitful and multiply and fill the earth" (Genesis 1:28). But the account of Eve's creation doesn't emphasize Adam's need to procreate. It emphasizes instead his need for relationship.[2]

Vines ignores two important points. First, Genesis 2 is a reiteration of Genesis 1. In the first chapter, we get an overview of creation. In the second chapter, we get the same story from a different perspective. In other words, the creation of woman in Genesis 2 cannot be divorced from the creation of mankind in Genesis 1. Nor can the procreation mandate.

In order for mankind to fulfill the cultural mandate given in Genesis 1:28, John Currid notes that the two humans in the Garden of Eden "must be both male and female with the ability to procreate."[3] Nor is Currid alone in his assessment. Joseph Haroutunian expands on this observation, noting that Genesis 2:18 explains God's purpose in creating woman: "God wished the earth to be populated by men who would live together and create a society."[4] Keenly aware of criticisms like Vines's, he writes:

> Some may question whether God's purpose included off-spring; for the words say only that since it is not well for a man to be alone, a woman had to be created to be his

helpmate. But . . . when God took the first steps towards a human society, he intended the others to follow each in turn. We have then a general principle: man was created to be a social animal. Now since the human race could not exist without woman, no bond whatever in human relations is more sacred than that by which husband and wife unite to become one body and one soul.[5]

The second problem with Vines's argument is that he ignores important elements of the creation narrative in Genesis 2 that point to an even broader application of the procreation mandate.

Procreation Involves Intimacy between Husband and Wife

A common caricature of conservative Christian sexuality is the "reproduction only" mentality. In other words, people believe conservative Christians see sexual pleasure as sinful unless it is specifically tied to procreation. In fact, such an attitude is often referred to as "puritanical." While there may be Christians who think and act this way (I have never met one), they are not the norm, nor are they acting in accordance with the beautiful picture of human sexuality we find in Scripture. Yes, God gave us sex to make babies, but He also gave us sex to make love.

The Song of Solomon is the most sensual book in the Bible. Unfortunately, aside from the occasional use of, "My beloved is mine and I am his" (2:16), in wedding ceremonies, it is also one of the least-read (and often never-preached) books in the Bible. That is due in part to its poetic style. But for those who do bother to read it and to analyze its poetry, there can be no doubt that God's view of sex is definitely not "procreation only." Just a few verses are sufficient to make the point.

> You have captivated my heart, my sister, my bride; you have captivated my heart with one glance of your eyes, with one jewel of your necklace. How beautiful is your love, my sister, my bride! How much better is your love than wine, and the fragrance of your oils than any spice! Your lips drip nectar, my bride; honey and milk are under your tongue; the fragrance of your garments is like the fragrance of Lebanon. (Song of Solomon 4:9–11)

The overt references to her eyes, lips, tongue, and fragrance take the encounter beyond the purely procreative. Then Solomon's beloved responds in what can only be described as ecstasy:

> Awake, O north wind, and come, O south wind! Blow upon my garden, let its spices flow. Let my beloved come to his garden, and eat its choicest fruits. (Song of Solomon 4:16)

The sexual nature of this text is inescapable! The next verse depicts Solomon's response after the encounter: "I came to my garden, my sister, my bride, I gathered my myrrh with my spice, I ate my honeycomb with my honey, I drank my wine with my milk." This is followed by the "chorus" exclaiming approvingly, "Eat, friends, drink, and be drunk with love" (Song of Solomon 5:1)!

Nor is Song of Solomon the only place the Bible speaks of the pleasure of sex. Proverbs, for example, dispels the myth of

procreation only by alluding to, among other things, the pleasure a woman's breasts bring to her husband: "Let your fountain
be blessed, and rejoice in the wife of your youth, a lovely deer, a
graceful doe. Let her breasts fill you at all times with delight; be
intoxicated always in her love" (Proverbs 5:18–19). This is nota-
ble since a procreation-only view of sex would view a woman's
breasts as no more than a vehicle for feeding children.

Beyond these examples of the Bible's celebration of marital
intimacy, there are also other implications to be drawn from the
idea of procreation in the creation account. It promotes intimacy by virtue of the physical union it requires. God designed
man to reproduce through an intimate sexual union. The Bible
describes it poetically in its opening chapters:

> Therefore a man shall leave his father and his mother
> and hold fast to his wife, and they shall become one flesh.
> And the man and his wife were both naked and were not
> ashamed. (Genesis 2:24–25)

The idea of a one-flesh union between the man and the woman
implies procreation for sure. However, the Bible paints a much
bigger picture—not least of which is the complementary nature
of the male and female bodies. The Apostle Paul uses the negative example of being joined together with a prostitute to illustrate the point:

> Do you not know that your bodies are members of Christ?
> Shall I then take the members of Christ and make them
> members of a prostitute? Never! Or do you not know that
> he who is joined to a prostitute becomes one body with

her? For, as it is written, "The two will become one flesh." But he who is joined to the Lord becomes one spirit with him. (1 Corinthians 6:15–17)

The implication here is clear. The one-flesh union between a man and woman involves more than just the potential for pregnancy; it involves intimacy. Hence, there is neither a need nor a justification for separating the procreative nature of male/female intercourse from the intimacy sex was designed to provide.

Second, the biblical idea of procreation also promotes intimacy by virtue of the spiritual and emotional union involved. Despite recent trends that have reduced the significance of sex between two people to slightly more than a handshake, the idea of two "becoming one flesh" is much more than a physical reality: It is also spiritual and emotional.

[Jesus] answered, "Have you not read that he who created them from the beginning made them male and female, and said, 'Therefore a man shall leave his father and his mother and hold fast to his wife, and the two shall become one flesh'? So they are no longer two but one flesh. What therefore God has joined together, let not man separate." (Matthew 19:4–6)

Here, Jesus makes it clear that God is the author of marriage, that Genesis 2 teaches marriage is reserved for males and females, and that the one-flesh union is more than just physical. We know that married people do not literally join together and become another physical entity—but for that brief space in time during coitus, they actually are. But in stating, "What therefore God has joined together, let not man separate," our Lord is making it clear that the one-flesh union is an ongoing spiritual reality beyond that brief space in time—it is a covenantal bond established by God Himself. Hence, the procreative bond is about much more than making babies.

We see another picture of the spiritual and emotional intimacy involved in sex between a man and a woman in the biblical term "to know."

> Now Adam knew Eve his wife, and she conceived and bore Cain, saying, "I have gotten a man with the help of the LORD." (Genesis 4:1; see also 4:17, 25; 1 Samuel 1:19)

The verb "to know" is used idiomatically several times in the Hebrew Bible. It signifies much more than just intellectual activity. It has a broader scope, meaning "to have intimacy with" or to "experience" another person, particularly sexually.[6] In light of this, it is clear that the act of human procreation was designed to involve more than just pregnancy and reproduction.

Third, the biblical idea of procreation promotes intimacy because of the partnership required to raise and train children.

> So God created man in his own image, in the image of God he created him; male and female he created them. And God blessed them. And God said to them, "Be fruitful and multiply and fill the earth and subdue it, and have dominion over the fish of the sea and over the birds of the heavens and over every living thing that moves on the earth." (Genesis 1:27–28)

The mandate to "be fruitful and multiply" involves two clear, distinct, yet related elements. First, there is the command to "fill the earth." Second, there is the command to "subdue it." This second command requires more than simply having children. We hear this clearly in Paul's admonition, "Fathers, do not provoke your children to anger, but bring them up in the discipline and instruction of the Lord" (Ephesians 6:4). This idea is echoed throughout Scripture (see Genesis 18:19; Deuteronomy 4:9, 6:7, 11:19; Psalms 78:4; Proverbs 19:18, 22:6, and 29:17).

God gave us marriage to fill the earth with the *imago dei*. This points clearly and undeniably to male/female marriage. It is also a clear argument against forbidding marriage between people of various ethnicities. Unlike same-sex marriage advocates, those who advocated for interethnic marriages had Scripture (along with history and tradition) on their side. It is therefore illegitimate to equate the struggle for same-sex marriage with the struggle to end antimiscegenation laws. One was struggling against sin; the other, against God.

Illustration

Marriage was not only given for procreation, but for illustration. It displays for us the nature of a triune God, the relationship between Christ and the Church, and ultimately, our eschatological hope.

Divine Triunity

The triune God who has existed eternally in a perfect, harmonious relationship between Father, Son, and Spirit has made man in His image and likeness (Genesis 1:27). Later we read:

> The LORD God took the man and put him in the garden
> of Eden to work it and keep it. And the LORD God com-
> manded the man, saying, "You may surely eat of every
> tree of the garden, but of the tree of the knowledge of
> good and evil you shall not eat, for in the day that you eat
> of it you shall surely die." Then the LORD God said, "It is
> not good that the man should be alone; I will make him a
> helper fit for him." (Genesis 2:15–18)

The astute reader would quickly recognize the magnitude of this statement. In the previous chapter, the pattern was, "let there be ... then there was ... it was good" on every day of creation. It is punctuated on the sixth day when we read,

> And God saw everything that he had made, and behold,
> *it was very good.* And there was evening and there was
> morning, the sixth day. (Genesis 1:31; emphasis mine)

So when God suddenly says something is *not good*, we must pay attention.

The sequence of events is important. God makes man, puts him in the garden, then gives him the command not to eat from the Tree of the Knowledge of Good and Evil, lest he die. Only then does God observe that "it is not good that the man should be alone." This is important because the declaration of "not good" comes *before* the Fall. Consequently, whatever is *not good* is also not sin, since there was no sin at that time. The good spoken of here is not a moral good, but a philosophical one.

The triune God has created man in His image and likeness, and man is alone. In other words, the man made in God's image is incapable of reflecting the image of the triune God unless and until he is in relationship. And not just any relationship—a relationship that allows him to illustrate the reality of the triune God. In the Godhead, the Son is eternally begotten of the Father, and the Spirit proceeds from the Father and the Son. So God puts the man made in His image to sleep; from him will come the woman, and children will proceed from the union of the woman and the man. In a way, a human family is meant to reflect the godhead. We are a relational people made in the image of a relational God.

Of course, our families are broken, imperfect reflections of the perfect union of the godhead, but they are reflections nonetheless. The fact that we all fall short of this ideal is no excuse to downplay or abandon it. When we think of marriage, we must keep this ideal in mind, and when we consider alternative or competing definitions of marriage, we must recognize them as a frontal attack—not merely on tradition, but on God Himself. The idea of two men or two women serving as an appropriate substitute or alternative for this reality is unthinkable.

The Relationship between Christ and the Church

The most familiar image of biblical marriage is also the most controversial one. The bulk of that controversy can be summed up in three verses of Scripture:

> Wives, submit to your own husbands, as to the Lord. For the husband is the head of the wife even as Christ is the head of the church, his body, and is himself its Savior. Now as the church submits to Christ, so also wives should submit in everything to their husbands. (Ephesians 5:22–24)

"I do not know many feminists who hold the institution of marriage as radically negative or dangerous as I had in my past," writes Rosaria Butterfield, reflecting on her life as a feminist, lesbian women's studies professor.[7] Before her conversion, Butterfield viewed the institution of marriage "as dangerous and as something to be avoided."

> When the subject of "gay marriage" would come up among my friends, I would respond by asking, "Why add good people to a sick institution?"[8]

What caused such hostility? It was Butterfield's understanding of the traditional roles of men and women in marriage.

> When you come to Christian marriage from a feminist perspective, the most difficult idea to embrace is that of a husband's headship and a wife's submission. When I'm looking at this paradigm from a secular perspective, it smacks of the abuses of patriarchy.[9]

But Butterfield did not maintain this view. She was gloriously saved from her sin and transformed. She now sees this biblical reality in an entirely different light and has been happily married to a man for many years.

> Kent's headship and my submission has been a source of comfort and solidarity. When Christ is at the center of our marriage, Kent's headship and my submission has allowed us to be a functional team.[10]

This is Christian marriage in action. The Apostle Paul wrote:

> Husbands, love your wives, as Christ loved the church and gave himself up for her, that he might sanctify her, having cleansed her by the washing of water with the word, so that he might present the church to himself in splendor, without spot or wrinkle or any such thing, that she might be holy and without blemish. In the same way husbands should love their wives as their own bodies. He who loves his wife loves himself. For no one ever hated his own flesh, but nourishes and cherishes it, just as Christ does the church, because we are members of his body. "Therefore a man shall leave his father and mother and hold fast to his wife, and the two shall become one flesh." This mystery is profound, and I am saying that it refers to Christ and the church. However, let each one of you love his wife as himself, and let the wife see that she respects her husband. (Ephesians 5:25–33)

Clearly, God's intention for marriage includes illustrating His character and nature to the world. This is seen only in male/female marriage. Even couples beyond childbearing years can fulfill this purpose. However, a husband can only be a husband if he has a wife (and vice versa). Neither two husbands, nor two wives, could accurately depict the character and nature of the God who made them male and female in His own image—nor could men who identify as women, or women who identify as men.

However, marriage between people of different ethnicities can depict God's nature. Christ's union with His Bride will culminate in "a great multitude that no one could number, from every nation, from all tribes and peoples and languages, standing before the throne and before the Lamb" (Revelation 7:9).

Sanctification

In addition to procreation and illustration, God created marriage for the purpose of sanctification. The Greek term for sanctify, *hagiazō*, means to "set apart" for God's special use or "to make distinct from what is common."[11] More specifically, the term means to make one holy, set apart from sin. According to the Second London Baptist Confession of Faith:

> The dominion of the whole body of sin is destroyed, and the various evil desires that arise from it are more and more weakened and put to death. At the same time, those called and regenerated are more and more enlivened and strengthened in all saving graces so that they practice true holiness, without which no one will see the Lord. (2LBC XIII.1)

Thus, when we speak of sanctification as a purpose for marriage, we are speaking of marriage as a means of setting men and women apart from the dominion of sin and conforming them to the image of Christ. This happens in two particular ways.

A God-Honoring Outlet for Sexual Desire

The first and most direct way marriage contributes to sanctification is by providing a God-honoring outlet for sexual desires. The clearest biblical example of this is found in 1 Corinthians 7:1–5:

Now concerning the matters about which you wrote: "It is good for a man not to have sexual relations with a woman." But because of the temptation to sexual immorality, each man should have his own wife and each woman her own husband. The husband should give to his wife her conjugal rights, and likewise the wife to her husband. For the wife does not have authority over her own body, but the husband does. Likewise the husband does not have authority over his own body, but the wife does. Do not deprive one another, except perhaps by agreement for a limited time, that you may devote yourselves to prayer; but then come together again, so that Satan may not tempt you because of your lack of self-control. (1 Corinthians 7:1–5)

There are three key distinctives in the text as it relates to the sanctifying nature of marriage. First, Paul references the sinful nature of sex outside of marriage. Second, he references the mutual expression of conjugal rights in marriage. Third, he warns against depriving one another of those conjugal rights. Much could be said about each of these, but for our purposes, allow me to emphasize one simple truth: Human sexuality is made holy to the degree that it takes place within the context and confines of a relationship established and set apart by God.

Evangelicals who wish to include same-sex marriage in this category have to prove that 1) homosexuality is not inherently sinful, and 2) God's design for sex has nothing to do with the natural, complementary, procreative nature of the male-female union. In their attempt to do so, they lower the bar, often reducing the sinfulness of sex not to that which fails to reflect God's design and purpose, but to that which involves "good intent" or does no harm. Matthew Vines offers a good example of the latter.

> With most sins, it wasn't hard to pinpoint the damage they cause. Adultery violates a commitment to your spouse. Lust objectifies others. Gossip degrades people. But committed same-sex relationships didn't fit this pattern. Not only were they not harmful to anyone, they were characterized by positive motives and traits instead, like faithfulness, commitment, mutual love, and self-sacrifice.[12]

Vines views man's "positive motives and traits" as sufficient to sanctify his sexual activity. But what about the physical harm of deviant sexual practices?

Chief among these harmful practices is anal intercourse. Interestingly, that is exactly what Vines and others are arguing in favor of, though they *never* mention it. Terms like "homosexual" and "same-sex attraction" sound harmless enough. Used in conjunction with terms like "loving" and "committed," they sound downright positive. However, use the term "anal intercourse" and the thin veneer of respectability is shot to shreds, leaving only the degrading and damaging facts. To say that anal intercourse is "harmful" is a gross understatement. Allow me to illustrate.

Former surgeon general C. Everett Koop noted as far back as 1990 that "condoms provide some protection, but anal intercourse is simply too dangerous to practice."[13] Dr. Ruth Jacobs, an infectious disease expert who was trained at the National Institutes of Health, wrote in a letter to a local newspaper in Montgomery County, Maryland, in 2005 that "due to anatomy and physiology, anal sex has been estimated to be at least twenty times riskier than vaginal"[14] for the person on the receiving end. For one thing, condoms are more likely to break during anal sex than the vaginal variety,[15] and secondly, as Jacobs told the Montgomery County school board,

> feces are filled with dangerous pathogens: salmonella, shigella, amoeba, hepatitis A, B, and C, giardia, campylobacter, and others. These organisms and others can be transmitted during anal sex or oral-anal contact and the consequences can be much more serious than a few days of vomiting.[16]

How can such a thing be considered harmless?

The FDA also warned against anal sex as early as 1990, stating that even when condoms are used, it

> is very risky because it can cause tissue in the rectum to tear and bleed. These tears allow disease germs to pass more easily from one partner to the other.[17]

And this is assuming that condoms are used at all. In most instances, they are not. According to a study published in the *Journal of Public Health Management Practices* in 2022,

> Statistics from meta-analyses [conducted between 2012 and 2017] showed that the rates of consistent condom use were 28 percent among HIV-infected and 29 percent among uninfected gay men in the United States.[18]

Dr. John Potterat is one of the country's leading epidemiologists. For nearly thirty years, he was the director of a clinic treating sexually transmitted diseases and AIDS in Colorado, and he has authored hundreds of scholarly articles on that topic. He summed up the dangers of anal intercourse better than most when he told his kids, "The anus is an exit, not an entrance." As Grossman explains, the reason he told them this is that

> The anal lining is only one cell thick . . . there is no lubrication, so tissue microtears are common, and access to the bloodstream is easy. Unlike the vagina, nature put a tight sphincter at the entrance of the anus. It's there for a reason: Keep out![19]

No wonder gay men and bisexuals have the highest rates of sexually transmitted disease! Despite comprising only 2 percent of the U.S. population, gay men

> accounted for 59% of new HIV infections and 62% of cases of early syphilis in 2009 [due to unprotected anal sex]. The Centers for Disease Control and Prevention (CDC) estimates that HIV and early syphilis rates among MSM are >40 times higher than those among heterosexuals.[20]

And this is to say nothing of issues like rectal incontinence and other natural consequences.[21]

The apostle's warning in Romans 1 rings true:

> For this reason God gave them up to dishonorable passions. For their women exchanged natural relations for

those that are contrary to nature; and the men likewise gave up natural relations with women and were consumed with passion for one another, men committing shameless acts with men *and receiving in themselves the due penalty for their error.* (Romans 1:26–27; emphasis mine)

Sex is a glorious gift from our good God. In its proper context, it is holy. Outside of that context, however, it becomes something altogether different—something unholy, unhealthy, unnatural, and dishonorable. Codifying such relationships into law is the ultimate act of rebellion against a holy God.

CHAPTER 11

And Such Were Some of You

I am often asked why this issue matters so much to me. That question is hard to answer. This issue concerns me as a cultural apologist and an American. But perhaps my greatest area of concern is pastoral. I have walked with people as they struggled with sexual sins of various kinds. However, sexual sins related to LGBTQIA2S+ are unique—not because of their practice, but their acceptance.

When a Christian man or woman is struggling with same-sex attraction, that struggle is compounded by the broader culture's insistence that a) it is an immutable sexual orientation, and b) it is not only impossible, but actually evil to even try to change that orientation. When a family is wrestling with what to do about a child who has come home from school identifying as transgender, it is a heavy burden to bear. When that family has to weigh their Christian convictions against an entire industry of professionals who have deemed "gender-affirming care" as the only acceptable path, the burden goes from heavy to unbearable in a hurry.

What makes all this so frustrating is the fact that I (and many others) know better. I know people who have walked away from these lifestyles. There are ex-gays and detransitioners out there. In this chapter, I want to offer hope to those who wrestle with these feelings, thoughts, and desires, and those walking alongside them. The world, the flesh, and the devil are all lying!

> Or do you not know that the unrighteous will not inherit the kingdom of God? Do not be deceived: neither the sexually immoral, nor idolaters, nor adulterers, nor men who practice homosexuality, nor thieves, nor the greedy, nor drunkards, nor revilers, nor swindlers will inherit the kingdom of God. *And such were some of you.* But you were washed, you were sanctified, you were justified in the name of the Lord Jesus Christ and by the Spirit of our God. (1 Corinthians 6:9–11; emphasis mine)

I'm about to tell you the stories of two people—but they are far, far from the only two. If you would like to read about others, or if you or someone you love is struggling with issues of sexual and/or gender identity, please visit www.ChangedMovement.com.

Rosaria Butterfield

Rosaria Butterfield holds a Ph.D. in English literature and critical theory from the Ohio State University. In the 1990s, she was a lesbian, a professor of English and women's studies at Syracuse University, and a gay activist. Of her academic life, Butterfield notes,

My historical interests in nineteenth-century literature were grounded in the philosophical and political world-views of Freud, Marx, and Darwin. My primary field was Critical Theory—also known as postmodernism. My specialty was Queer Theory (a postmodern form of gay and lesbian studies).[1]

She and her lover belonged to a Unitarian Universalist Church, where Butterfield coordinated the "Welcoming Committee"—the church's gay and lesbian advocacy group.[2] Her activism was rooted in her conviction that sexual identity is a key component of diversity. She was a very happy, well-informed lesbian with a heterosexual past. She received her primary and secondary education in Roman Catholic schools, and from the ages of twenty-two to twenty-eight, she was involved in heterosexual relationships. However, she says, "at the same time an undercurrent of longing began to insert itself into my relationships with women."[3]

Butterfield believed her lesbian lifestyle was actually a superior moral choice. She also grew to believe that her Roman Catholic education was rooted in anti-intellectualism and superstition.

In 1997, she published an article in the *Syracuse Post Gazette* on Promise Keepers, the Christian men's movement that was sweeping the nation at the time; the ministry had come to town to hold a large event in the stadium on campus. Butterfield was waging war against "the patriarchy," so Promise Keepers was a natural target. She had also recently coauthored the university's domestic partnership policy, so she was already in the news, and the paper was eager to post her piece. An elder at the Syracuse Reformed Presbyterian Church took Butterfield's op-ed to

Pastor Ken Smith and said, "We need to shut this woman up; she's trouble."

But Smith had a different idea: He invited Butterfield to his home for dinner. At the time, she was writing a book on the religious right and had begun to read the Bible for her research.

Butterfield had been separating the barrage of letters responding to her article into two piles on her desk: fan mail and hate mail. But Smith's letter defied such easy categorization. He wasn't disagreeing or arguing with her as much as he was urging her to examine her underlying worldview assumptions and perhaps consider his.

Butterfield saw Smith's invitation as an opportunity for free research for her book. The result was a pleasant evening with Smith and his wife, Floy, having fruitful conversation that turned into a real friendship.

Two things Smith did—or rather, didn't do—during that first dinner intrigued Butterfield. First, he did not share the Gospel with her. Second, he did not invite her to church. She was shocked! He didn't treat Rosaria as a project, but as a neighbor. Butterfield and the Smiths went on to have many more dinners. They exchanged books, met each other's friends, and had many open and frank discussions about the Bible, sexuality, politics, and many other issues. "Ken's God was holy and firm, but full of mercy," Butterfield later wrote.[4]

At one of the weekly LGBT gatherings at her home, one of her transgendered friends—a former Presbyterian minister—remarked, "This Bible reading is changing you. I prayed that God would change me, but He didn't. If you want, I will pray for you."[5]

The next day, Butterfield found a milk crate on her front porch overflowing with her transgendered friend's old theological books. And she found herself reading them not only for her research, but for her own curiosity.

"I didn't come to Christ because I thought coming to Christ was a good deal," Butterfield later wrote. "I didn't come to Christ because I stopped loving my girlfriend, or because I stopped loving being a lesbian. I came to Christ because of who Christ is."

Butterfield found the root of her sin and repented of it. Her explanation of this process is worth noting:

> When we call sin sin and repent of it, we honor God's authority. Getting to a posture of repentance, though, is often its own battle, as the flesh cries out for the forbidden object and the heart and mind owned by Jesus beg for deliverance. Christ is in us and he is for us in this battle. Because repentance is actually the threshold to God.[6]

Butterfield goes on to direct those who struggle with homosexual desires:

> This is a hard and a heavy cross to bear. I know this. I also know that if you are in Christ, Jesus will bear the heavier part of this burden. Crosses are not curses.

To the rest of the audience, she warns against thinking that homosexuality is different from other sins or that "its solution is heterosexuality." The solution to all sins, she noted, "is Christ's atoning blood."

> In Christ we are new creatures. In Christ we have a new will and heart and affections for God's word and his will.

We are redeemed men and women who have been buried with Christ through baptism into death. And we are no longer slaves to the sin that once defined us. Although likely, it still knows our names and addresses.[7]

At some point, her desire to become a godly woman "bled into the desire to become the godly wife of a godly husband."[8] And that is exactly what Rosaria Butterfield became. The woman who admits, "I do not know many feminists who hold the institution of marriage as radically negative or dangerous as I had in my past,"[9] is now married to a Presbyterian pastor. She is also an adoptive parent and a homeschooling mother. Oh, and she continues to serve as an English professor . . . at a Christian university.

Christopher Yuan

Christopher Yuan says he was not always Christian.[10] He was born in a conservative Chinese-American home in 1970 and grew up in Chicago. Like many young men, he was exposed to pornography at a young age—nine—and began wrestling with his sexuality.

Yuan's story is anything but typical. He served in the United States Marine Corps Reserve, then studied dentistry. During that time, he "came out" to his parents, shocking them deeply. Things only got more complicated when both his parents subsequently became Christians.

Yuan eventually dropped out of dental school and lived what he refers to as "a life of partying and drugs," including sex with lots of men.[11] Eventually, he moved from using drugs to dealing them.

When his parents visited him, he ended up kicking them out of his home—not because they preached at him, but because, he said, they so radiated Christ and were so obviously changed, that he found their very presence offensive.[12] Before leaving, Yuan's father gave him a Bible, which he threw in the trash. He wanted nothing to do with his parents or their Christianity.[13]

Yuan's parents enlisted over one hundred prayer warriors to join them in contending for him in the spiritual realm; his mom fasted every Monday for seven years and at one point went on a thirty-nine-day fast. She would often spend hours praying and reading Scripture as she agonized over her son's lost condition. She prayed, "God, do whatever it takes . . ." knowing it would take a miracle.[14]

The miracle came in the form of twelve federal agents, two German shepherd drug dogs, and the Atlanta police banging on Yuan's door after he had received a large shipment of drugs in the late 1990s. Yuan, charged with possession of the equivalent of 9.1 tons of marijuana, was sentenced to six years in prison.[15]

While serving his sentence, Yuan walked by a trashcan one day and thought, "That's my life—trash!" Then he spotted something in the trash: a Gideons New Testament. He took it back to his cell, and that night he read Mark's gospel—not because he was interested, but because he was bored. Nonetheless, those words began to convict him.[16]

A couple of weeks later, Yuan found out he was HIV positive. As he lay in his bunk, he looked up at the ceiling, where someone had written, "If you're bored, read Jeremiah 29:11." He found the verse, which reads, "For I know the plans I have for you, declares the LORD, plans for welfare and not for evil, to give you a future and a hope." Those words gave him hope.[17]

Yuan's transformation was gradual. He kept reading the Bible and finding hope as he learned God loved him unconditionally. However, he also kept reading passages that condemn homosexuality. That bothered him, so he continued to search the Scriptures for something that would affirm his homosexuality. One day, he asked the prison chaplain for help. The chaplain told him the Bible did not condemn same-sex relationships, and even gave him a book that made the same argument.[18]

Yuan didn't have any kind of theological training, but as he took that book in one hand and the Bible in the other, he could tell both the book and the chaplain were distorting the clear meaning of Scripture. He put the book away and continued to search the Bible for something that would affirm his homosexuality, to no avail. At that point, Yuan realized he was at a crossroad. He could either abandon God and live as a gay man pursuing same-sex relationships—thus allowing his attractions to dictate not only who he was, but how he lived—or he would abandon pursuing same-sex relationships by freeing himself from homosexuality and live as a follower of Jesus Christ.[19]

By God's grace, he followed Jesus.

He realized that unconditional love did not mean unconditional approval of his behavior. He learned that his identity was not gay. It was not even ex-gay; it was a child of God. He learned that the opposite of homosexuality was not heterosexuality; it was holiness. He learned that even men with opposite-sex attractions had to pursue holiness. He learned that heterosexuality was the right direction, but not the right goal. Yuan later wrote,

God never says, "Be heterosexual for I am heterosexual."
Nor does he say, "Be homosexual for I am homosexual."

Both are Freudian, secular categories, not biblical categories. God says, "Be holy for I am holy."[20]

God was revealing this throughout Yuan's time in prison.
Eventually, by God's grace, his sentence was reduced from six
years to three. During that time, God called him to full-time
Christian ministry.[21]

After his release in 2001, Yuan applied to Moody Bible
Institute in his hometown of Chicago and was accepted for the
fall term. His three letters of reference were from a prison chaplain, a prison guard, and another inmate. He was accepted to
Moody. He completed his master's degree in biblical exegesis in
2005 and earned a doctor of ministry degree in 2014. He then
coauthored a memoir with his mother, *Out of a Far Country:
A Gay Son's Journey to God. A Broken Mother's Search for
Hope.*[22]

Answering Objections to Such Testimonies

Whenever I share such stories, I am keenly aware of the objections they raise. Nevertheless, I share them. I know they don't
settle the issue, but the objections they raise are as helpful to my
purposes as the stories themselves. There are two main objections: 1) these people were never really gay, and 2) these people
really are gay and just living in denial.

Both of these objections are rooted in the *a priori* commitment to the notion of immutable sexual orientation.

These People Were Never Really Gay

The objection goes something like this: If people like Butterfield
and Yuan were truly homosexual, then they would not have

reverted to heterosexuality. But does the argument have any merit?

The main problem with this objection is that is rooted in a double standard. It turns out, "live your truth" only works in one direction. For instance, the moment a person who has lived a heterosexual lifestyle comes out as gay, there is instant, unquestioning, euphoric celebration of their heroic decision to "live their truth." On the other hand, people who leave the homosexual lifestyle are often said never to have been gay at all. If sexual orientation is fixed and immutable, like race, then how could a heterosexual ever become homosexual? The answer: They couldn't. So when faced with this paradox, people will claim that the former homosexual was either mistaken about his/her identity or is lying about their change.

These People Are Just Denying Who They Really Are

Matthew Vines has a great deal to say about the failure of ex-gay ministries and how those failures prove his thesis on sexual orientation. "These 'ex-gay' organizations, for the most part, did not claim to be changing anyone's sexual orientation," he writes. "They focused instead on changing people's behavior."[23]

Note that Vines is begging the question. He assumes the truth of his foundational argument (i.e., sexual orientation is immutable) without offering a shred of evidence for it, then, based on that assertion, states that only behavior is changed when someone leaves that lifestyle. This is important to him because, in his estimation, sexual orientation removes the sinfulness from homosexuality. Hence, he can say, "For people who had been caught up in promiscuity, abusive relationships, or drug addictions, changing those behaviors was surely beneficial."[24] In other words, it is beneficial and legitimate for sinners to avoid sinful behavior even if the desires remain, but that is irrelevant for former homosexuals since "those changes had no bearing on their sexual orientation."[25] How does Vines know this? Because desire was still present, and, as so many people would have us believe, desire = orientation.

For Vines, this approach is unthinkable because it "places gay Christians who adhere to the traditional biblical interpretation in an agonizing, irresolvable tension"[26] resulting from the fact that "in order to truly flee from sin as well as the temptation to sin, [gay people] must constantly attempt what has proven impossible."[27] In other words, the testimonies above cannot possibly be accurate or true, because leaving homosexuality has been "proven" to be as impossible as a black person ceasing to be black! In fact, Vines makes the audacious claim that the only real way out for those who adhere to the "traditional biblical interpretation" is "to reconstitute themselves so they are no longer sexual beings at all."[28]

Presbyterian pastor Greg Johnson argues against "gay Christian" theology yet echoes Vines's view. "Jesus hasn't made me straight," he wrote in a *Christianity Today* article, "but he covers over my shame. Jesus really loves gay people."[29] In Johnson's view,

> The gospel doesn't erase this part of my story so much as it redeems it. My sexual orientation doesn't define me. It's not the most important or most interesting thing about me. It is the backdrop for that, the backdrop for the story of Jesus who rescued me.[30]

But is that what the evidence says?

In 2003, the late Columbia University psychiatrist Robert Spitzer published a paper in the *Archives of Sexual Behavior* that would most assuredly get him canceled today: "Can Some Gay Men and Lesbians Change Their Sexual Orientation? 200 Participants Reporting a Change from Homosexual to Heterosexual Orientation." Spitzer writes:

> Reports of complete change were uncommon. Female participants reported significantly more change than did male participants. Either some gay men and lesbians, following reparative therapy, actually change their predominantly homosexual orientation to a predominantly heterosexual orientation or some gay men and women construct elaborate self-deceptive narratives (or even lie) in which they claim to have changed their sexual orientation, or both. . . . For many reasons, it is concluded that the participants' self-reports were, by and large, credible and that few elaborated self-deceptive narratives or lied.[31]

Spitzer emphatically concluded: "Thus, there is evidence that change in sexual orientation following some form of reparative therapy does occur in some gay men and lesbians."[32]

Spitzer's findings are rare in today's academy, where even suggesting such research be done, much less coming to those conclusions, is considered homophobic and grounds for termination. Nevertheless, they are consistent with the Apostle Paul's statement in 1 Corinthians 6 cited at the beginning of this chapter. Moreover, it is even consistent with the findings of Alfred Kinsey, who noted that his research subjects displayed a tendency to move in and out of homosexuality.[33]

Vines compares homosexuality to other sins like "promiscuity, abusive relationships, or drug addictions." He argues that it is unfair and impossible to expect homosexuals to forego same-sex relationships, but fine to expect those who are promiscuous or addicted to drugs to change their behavior.[34] Interestingly, there is more evidence for an orientation toward drug addiction than there is for homosexuality; according to the American Psychological Association, "at least half of a person's susceptibility to drug addiction can be linked to genetic factors."[35] Yet, despite studying more than half a million people, scientists have not been able to identify any such genetic cause for homosexuality.[36]

Alcoholics Anonymous

This scientific evidence throws into particularly stark relief the difference between cultural reactions to reparative therapy aimed at helping people deal with their unwanted same-sex attractions and twelve-step programs that help people deal with their unwanted attractions to drugs and alcohol.

If you have a substance-abuse problem, everyone tells us, these programs are the answer: "The program works if you work it." The only problem is, the program doesn't work. At least, not for most people.

"AA has been the gold standard in drug and alcohol treatment for the better part of a century. Unless you've been living under a rock, you have heard of the program. What you probably haven't heard is there is a lack of evidence supporting its efficacy," write Lance and Zachary Dodes in their scathing exposé, *The Sober Truth*.[37] The book's subtitle says it all: *Debunking the Bad Science behind Twelve-Step Programs and the Rehab Industry*. The Dodeses have more than three decades of experience treating people with addiction. Their book is a thorough analysis of available data on the success of AA. Today, they write, "almost every treatment center, physician, and court system in the country uses this model." And this despite the fact that AA "has one of the worst success rates in all of medicine." How bad? The Dodeses put it "between 5 and 10 percent, hardly better than no treatment at all."[38]

But what about the constant bombardment on television shows, the referrals from medical professionals, and the testimonies of successful twelve-steppers? The problem, according to the Dodeses, is that "[m]ost studies of AA that purport to show its effectiveness are observational in nature, with no controls that might help us capably determine results."[39]

There is significant evidence that twelve-step programs have very limited success. Nevertheless, they are celebrated in the broader culture, trusted and relied upon to treat those struggling with addictions of various types from alcohol and narcotics to sex and gambling, and treated as sacred cows never to be questioned. Meanwhile, there are laws passed against treatments for people who wish to be free of their same-sex attractions, and much of that is based upon evidence of "limited success" and the religious nature of programs treating SSA. Ironically, both of these issues are inherent to AA.

AA's twelfth step involves both evangelism and a commitment to perpetual practice. Hence, AA's commitment to the concept of "once an addict, always an addict" and insistence that even those with decades of sobriety are still "recovering addicts." In other words, there is no "cure" in AA, only perpetual struggle to avoid the temptation that can strike at any moment.

Apply these same ideas to same-sex attraction, though, and the story changes instantly. For example, Canada's Bill C4, often seen as a harbinger of things to come in the U.S. and elsewhere, states that "Conversion therapy has been denounced by medical and psychological professionals as being ineffective and harmful." The bill then goes on to describe the supposed harm:

> The harms that can be caused by conversion therapy include distress, anxiety, depression, stigma, shame, negative self-image, a feeling of personal failure, difficulty sustaining relationships, sexual dysfunction and having serious thoughts or plans of—or attempting—suicide.[40]

Anybody who has worked with people struggling with addiction to drugs, alcohol, or anything they desperately want to be rid of has watched them deal with "distress, anxiety, depression, stigma, shame, negative self-image, a feeling of personal failure, difficulty sustaining relationships, sexual dysfunction and having serious thoughts or plans of—or attempting—suicide."

Why don't we conclude, in light of these realities, that addiction is an "orientation" that ought to be respected? Why, in light of the limited success of twelve-step programs, don't we pass laws against them, or at least condemn them? Is it because there is some hard evidence to support the immutability of sexual orientation? Is it because we view the harms of drug and alcohol addictions as more severe than those associated with homosexual lifestyles?[41] Or is it because AA's Twelve Steps, its expressions, and unique lexicon have found their way into the public discourse in a way that few other "brands" could ever match?[42]

Our War with Sexual Sin

I don't say any of this to condemn those who use AA or any other program to help them in their struggle. I'm simply pointing out the hypocrisy of saying reparative therapy (often called "conversion therapy" in an attempt to disparage the practice) should be banned based on religious content or success rates. Moreover, the fact that one struggles with sin is no reason to capitulate to the sin. Like the abuse of drugs, alcohol, gambling, etc., sexual sin has far-reaching implications and consequences. Embracing the idea of "sexual minorities" will not bring about a rise in God-honoring relationships. On the contrary, it will bring about degradation and despair.

"What good Christians don't realize," writes Rosaria Butterfield, "is that sexual sin is not recreational sex gone overboard. Sexual sin is predatory. It won't be 'healed' by redeeming the context or the genders." She concludes, "Sexual sin must simply be killed. What is left of your sexuality after this annihilation is up to God. But healing, to the sexual sinner, is death: nothing more and nothing less."[43] This is a complete departure from the immutable sexual orientation argument.

Nor does Butterfield see the war against same-sex attraction as evidence of the sanctity of the same. She writes, "too many young Christian fornicators plan that marriage will redeem their sin. Too many young Christian masturbators plan that marriage will redeem their patterns. Too many young Christian internet pornographers think that having legitimate sex will take away the desire to have illicit sex." How right she is! But this thinking is flawed, and it has far-reaching implications. That is why "the marriages that result from this line of thinking are dangerous places."[44]

The sexual minority movement presents itself as a collection of people who are oppressed by society's norms and expectations. Leaving that question aside, how about this one: What if people like me—people who hold fast to biblical, traditional morality—believe that those who identify as "sexual minorities" are being oppressed by their own desires? What does it say about people who condemn us and demand that we abandon our sincerely held beliefs in the name of respecting, well, sincerely held beliefs? If I believe someone is driving headlong toward a cliff, will you condemn me for pleading with that person to stop and turn around? Yet that is exactly what is happening in this current cultural moment. People who believe that legalizing same-sex marriage, transitioning children, queering curricula, torturing the English language, and all the rest of the madness is causing great harm on both an individual and a societal level are being vilified and canceled in the name of tolerance. One wonders what this new tolerance will refuse to tolerate next.

Conclusion

Writing this book has been one of the most challenging and emotionally draining undertakings of my life. I have grown weary of being accused of catastrophism, homophobia, fascism, and plain old hatred in the course of the twenty years that have passed since I first began speaking about it. I have faced protests at live events, threats of violence, and censure of various types. I also have grown weary of reading, hearing, and seeing things that grieve my soul as I researched this topic.

I started teaching and speaking on this topic following the Prop 8 battle in California in 2008 and wrote a proposal and sample chapters for a book in 2010. (Publishers wouldn't touch it with a ten-foot pole.) As a result, there are things I wrote about then as warnings of what *could* happen that turned into the explanations in this book of what *did* happen. For example, back in 2008, even California couldn't pass a same-sex marriage bill. So when I addressed the issue in lectures, sermons, or other venues, I was accused of catastrophism when I warned that the march towards same-sex marriage was gaining momentum. Seven years later, *Obergefell* made same-sex marriage the law of the land in all fifty states. What's worse, eight years later, most Christians have come to view same-sex marriage as a done deal and therefore no longer see a reason to press the issue. Others have fully embraced the "open and affirming" position of the United Methodist Church (and other denominations). And what sane person back in 2008 would have predicted that we would have drag queen story hour at public libraries, queer clubs and pornographic books in primary schools, men competing with women in sports at every level, doctors recommending the chemical castration and genital mutilation of minors, and Supreme Court nominees not being able define what a woman is?

Another challenge is trying to explain to people on either side of the issue why this matters so much. From one side, I hear, "Why should you care what people do in the privacy of their own bedrooms?" or, "What could possibly be wrong with people loving each other?" From the other side, I get, "The court has spoken, and same-sex marriage is the law of the land. Why are you still tilting at that windmill?" Others ask, "Why not leave the political stuff alone and just focus your efforts on preaching the Gospel?" Those are all valid questions. I have answered most of them in the pages above, but let's revisit a few.

Questions about human sexuality matter because what God says matters, whether we agree with it or not. The first six verses of Psalm 2 put the matter into perspective: "Why do the nations rage and the peoples plot in vain" (Psalm 2:1)? The psalmist goes on to describe the attitude of the men of every age who desire to rid themselves of God's decrees:

The kings of the earth set themselves, and the rulers take counsel together, against the LORD and against his

> Anointed, saying, "Let us burst their bonds apart and cast
> away their cords from us." (Psalm 2:2–3)

The Lord is not fazed by man's rebellion. On the contrary, "He
who sits in the heavens laughs; the Lord holds them in derision"
(Psalm 2:4). Why? Because God is not running for office! He is
the sovereign ruler of the universe and needs permission from
no man.

> Then he will speak to them in his wrath, and terrify them
> in his fury, saying, "As for me, I have set my King on Zion,
> my holy hill." (Psalm 2:5–6)

Of course, this does not mean that God will necessarily adjudi-
cate matters immediately, or even on this side of eternity. What
it does mean is that God is God, and we disregard Him at our
own peril. If I believe this—and I do—the only loving response
is to call sinners to repent.

Second, no matter how often people have claimed that the
questions about "sexual minorities" were about people doing
what they do "in the privacy of their bedrooms," those issues
were never going to remain private. From the beginning, it has
been about forcing people to embrace and celebrate sexual deviance and marginalizing those who refuse to do so. From forcing
little girls to accept men intruding into their public restrooms
and competing against boys in their sports, to forcing churches
to perform same-sex ceremonies and refrain from preaching the
Bible's position on homosexuality, the idea that this was ever
about private behavior has been disproved many times over. If
you don't believe me, go to a gay pride parade. In fact, you don't

have to do that—just turn on the television, do some online shopping, or watch the news during the month of June, and the façade of "privacy" will quickly disappear. The public nature of the LGBTQIA2S+ movement has consequences for everyone— whether we agree with it or not.

What is ultimately wrong with the idea of celebrating "people loving each other" is that it creates a new moral standard, which is no standard at all. It redefines "love" as anything that brings one pleasure. It redefines "hate" as anything that argues for a moral standard other than hedonism. It redefines "evil" as anyone who believes there is such a thing, and "extremism" as any view to the right of Karl Marx. And that's to say nothing of its redefinition of men and women and its obliteration of pronouns.

I do not wish to police anybody's intimate relationships but my own. But I am very concerned about the culture my nine children and three grandchildren (so far) are inheriting. I am concerned about the fact that they will likely be forced to capitulate to this new sexual morality or forego significant opportunities in education, civil or military service, and much of the job market. I am concerned about an entertainment industry that portrays sexual minorities as the focal point of every story while marginalizing traditional, biblical Christianity. I am not concerned that these things are too big for God to handle; I simply want the best for my children . . . and for yours.

Ultimately, I am concerned because this new morality will eventually devour everything in its path. Today, even left-wing, traditional feminists are considered fascists because they refuse to bow the knee and confess, "Trans women are women." What on earth will tomorrow bring? How long before we have crossed the

Rubicon and there is nothing left in our wake but a generation of men and women whose lives have been devastated by their pursuit of more and greater perversions all looking back at us—their forefathers—and asking, "Why didn't you protect us from this?!"

I hope we have a better answer to give them than the one that seems likely right now. And I hope we have a better future to offer them than the present in which we are currently living.

So what should we do?

We Must Protect Our Children

In July 2021, a video surfaced that caused quite a stir. "A Message from the Gay Community"[1] was a song performed by the San Francisco Gay Men's Chorus. What was so alarming about the video? The song's "hook" was the line, "We'll convert your children." While the group claimed the video was satirical, the lyrics reveal "many a truth spoken in jest." The truth is revealed in lines like:

> *You think we're sinful*
> *You fight against our rights*
> *You say we all lead lives you can't respect.*
> *But you're just frightened*
> *You think that we'll corrupt your kids*
> *If our agenda goes unchecked.*
> *Funny—just this once*
> *You're correct.*

Nor are these the most haunting lyrics:

> *We'll convert your children*

Happens bit by bit,
Quietly and subtly
And you will barely notice it.
You can keep them from disco,
Warn about San Francisco,
Make 'em wear pleated pants, we don't care.
We'll convert your children . . .
We'll make them tolerant and fair.

Just like you worried
They'll change their group of friends,
You won't approve of where they go at night to protest.
And you'll be disgusted
When they start learning things online that you kept far from
    their sight (like information) . . .

We'll convert your children, yes we will!
Reaching one and all
There's really no escaping it
'Cause even Grandma likes RuPaul.
The world's getting kinder
Gen Z's gayer than Grindr
Learn to love, learn to vote, face your fate
We'll convert your children
Someone's gotta teach them not to hate.

We're coming for them.
We're coming for your children . . .
The gay agenda is coming home.
The gay agenda is here.

This is not satire! This is speaking the quiet part out loud. If you've been paying attention, you'll notice that this is a clear reference to the concept of "conversion" in Kirk and Madsen's propaganda strategy. And it is exactly what is happening in our schools. Unfortunately, it is also happening in many churches.

Dear friend, don't sleep on this! We must be vigilant and protect our children from this onslaught. Few things are spoken of more harshly in Scripture than those who cause little ones to sin:

> "Whoever receives one such child in my name receives me, but whoever causes one of these little ones who believe in me to sin, it would be better for him to have a great millstone fastened around his neck and to be drowned in the depth of the sea." (Matthew 18:5–6)

We Must Celebrate, Cherish, and Promote (True) Marriage

> Let marriage be held in honor among all, and let the marriage bed be undefiled, for God will judge the sexually immoral and adulterous. (Hebrews 13:4)

With these words, the writer of Hebrews reminds us of at least three things. First, marriage, as God designed it, is honorable. Second, sex, as God designed it, is holy. Third, all those who dishonor marriage and sex by pursuing either in a manner not prescribed by God will incur God's judgment. The Apostle Paul makes the point even clearer in 1 Thessalonians 4 when he writes:

For this is the will of God, your sanctification: that you abstain from sexual immorality; that each one of you know how to control his own body in holiness and honor, not in the passion of lust like the Gentiles who do not know God; see that no one transgress and wrong his brother in this matter, because the Lord is an avenger in all these things, as we told you beforehand and solemnly warned you. For God has not called us for impurity, but in holiness. (vv. 3–7)

The apostle concludes his admonition by reminding us that these words are not mere opinion: "Therefore whoever disregards this, disregards not man but God, who gives his Holy Spirit to you" (v. 8). This last point is of the utmost importance. Neither you nor I have the authority to insist on our moral preference or opinion. There is a God who created the world, and we are accountable to Him. We don't get to define marriage or the parameters around human sexuality. And for those who insist on using the transgressions of some Christians as justification to jettison Christian morality, know that you are not the first to attempt to do so. The Scriptures anticipate such objections and offer a response: "What if some were unfaithful? Does their faithlessness nullify the faithfulness of God? By no means! Let God be true though every one were a liar, as it is written, 'That you may be justified in your words, and prevail when you are judged'" (Romans 3:3–4). Marriage is honorable, not *because* of the way men represent the institution, but *in spite of* it.

I am a flawed, imperfect husband, married to a flawed, imperfect wife, and we have a flawed, imperfect marriage. The good news is, our marriage is not an end in itself; it is a temporal expression of an eschatological hope. There is a perfect Marriage to which our marriage points, and for which we and every other imperfect sinner wait eagerly:

> Then I heard what seemed to be the voice of a great multitude, like the roar of many waters and like the sound of mighty peals of thunder, crying out, "Hallelujah! For the Lord our God the Almighty reigns. Let us rejoice and exult and give him the glory, for the marriage of the Lamb has come, and his Bride has made herself ready; it was granted her to clothe herself with fine linen, bright and pure"— for the fine linen is the righteous deeds of the saints. And the angel said to me, "Write this: Blessed are those who are invited to the marriage supper of the Lamb." And he said to me, "These are the true words of God." (Revelation 19:6–9)

We Must Be Willing to Suffer as Strangers and Aliens

Perhaps the most difficult part of all of this is the fact that the message I have outlined in this book is foreign to some, reprehensible to many, and extreme to most. Argue for a form of marriage that goes against the Bible and the entire history of Western civilization and you're "progressive." Argue for the institution that has served as the foundation of every civilization in the history of mankind and you're a "right-wing extremist" or a "fascist." But this should not surprise anybody who is familiar with the Scriptures. The Apostle Peter, writing to the Christian diaspora in his first epistle, was addressing this reality when he wrote,

> Beloved, I urge you as sojourners and exiles to abstain from the passions of the flesh, which wage war against your soul. Keep your conduct among the Gentiles honorable, so that when they speak against you as evildoers, they may see your good deeds and glorify God on the day of visitation. (1 Peter 2:11–12)

The modern expression of "calling us evildoers" is branding us as right-wing extremists or fascists. But our task remains the same: We are called to "keep our conduct . . . honorable" so that when they brand us with epithets, they may see our good deeds and glorify God. But that is easier said than done. Nobody wants to be hated and called names. That's why we need the encouragement and admonition that comes later in Peter's letter:

> Now who is there to harm you if you are zealous for what is good? But even if you should suffer for righteousness' sake, you will be blessed. Have no fear of them, nor be troubled, but in your hearts honor Christ the Lord as holy, always being prepared to make a defense to anyone who asks you for a reason for the hope that is in you; yet do it with gentleness and respect, having a good conscience, so that, when you are slandered, those who revile your good behavior in Christ may be put to shame. For it is better to suffer for doing good, if that should be God's will, than for doing evil. (1 Peter 3:13–17)

We Must Be Ready to Give an Answer

I hope you caught the key line above. "Always being prepared to make a defense to anyone who asks you for a reason for the hope that is in you." That doesn't mean we have to be ready to win every argument or "destroy" every opponent. It simply means we must be ready to explain what we believe and why. We must be ready to tell those who hate us and the God in whose name we speak why it is that we are willing to live as strangers and aliens. We must be ready and willing to gently, respectfully, and clearly explain how we were lost sinners who were rescued by the grace of God through the person and work of Christ. We must be ready to explain how the cross of Christ is our only hope of forgiveness and our only claim to righteousness.

One of the most famous lines Dr. Martin Luther King Jr. ever uttered was his quote of Amos 5:24: "We will not be satisfied until 'justice rolls down like waters, and righteousness like a mighty stream.'"[2] But how many people know the context of those words? How many know that, in using that quote, King was not advocating for America to act like a "secular democracy," but for it to return to its foundation of biblical morality? If they did, I find it hard to believe that they would try to tie that movement to one that despises the God of the Bible and mocks the morality He requires. Perhaps we need to visit Amos's warning again:

> "I hate, I despise your feasts, and I take no delight in your solemn assemblies. Even though you offer me your burnt offerings and grain offerings, I will not accept them; and the peace offerings of your fattened animals, I will not look upon them. Take away from me the noise of your songs; to the melody of your harps I will not listen. But let justice roll down like waters, and righteousness like an ever-flowing stream." (Amos 5:21–24)

Endnotes

Introduction

1 Casey Harper, "'No Chance of Winning': Four Female Athletes Challenge High School Transgender Policy," The Center Square, September 30, 2022, https://www.thecentersquare.com/national/article _eef6fe80-40d4-11ed-b716-ef3255a8ad7e.html.

2 Katie Barnes, "Amid Protests, Penn Swimmer Lia Thomas Becomes First Known Transgender Athlete to Win Division I National Championship," ESPN.com, March 17, 2022, https://www.espn.com/college-sports /story/_/id/33529775/amid-protests-pennsylvania-swimmer-lia-thomas -becomes-first-known-transgender-athlete-win-division-national -championship.

3 Bhavesh Purohit, "When Transgender Fighter Fallon Fox Broke Her Opponent's Skull in MMA Fight," Sportskeeda, September 30, 2021, https://www.sportskeeda.com/mma/news-when-transgender-fighter -fallon-fox-broke-opponent-s-skull-mma-fight.

4 The Associated Press, "First Openly Transgender Olympians Are Competing in Tokyo," NBC News, July 26, 2021, https://www.nbcnews .com/nbc-out/out-news/first-openly-transgender-olympians-are -competing-tokyo-rcna1507.

5 Cyd Zeigler, "4 Myths and Flat-Out Lies Being Told about Trans MMA Fighter Fallon Fox," OutSports, February 22, 2021, https://www.out sports.com/2021/2/22/22296155/fallon-fox-trans-mma-fighter-lie -inclusion-misleading.

6 Samantha Kamman, "Man Crowned Winner of Miss Netherlands Beauty Pageant," Christian Post, July 12, 2023, https://www.christian post.com/news/biological-male-wins-miss-netherlands-beauty-pageant .html.

7   USA Today, "Sen. Blackburn Asks Supreme Court Nominee to Define 'Woman'|USA Today," YouTube, March 23, 2022, https://www.youtube.com/watch?v=BWtGzJxiONU.

8   *What Is a Woman?*, The Daily Wire, https://www.dailywire.com/videos/what-is-a-woman.

9   Michael Clements, "Oklahoma Governor Issues Executive Order Defining Biological Sex," *Epoch Times,* August 2, 2023, https://www.theepochtimes.com/us/oklahoma-governor-issues-executive-order-defining-biological-sex-5441040.

10 Anthony Kennedy, *Obergefell v. Hodges*, Supreme Court of the United States, June 26, 2015, https://www.law.cornell.edu/supremecourt/text/14-556#writing-14-556_OPINION_3.

11 Jeremiah Ho, "Once We're Done Honeymooning: *Obergefell v. Hodges*, Incrementalism, and Advances for Sexual Orientation Anti-Discrimination," *Kentucky Law Journal* 104, no. 2 (2015–2016): 283, https://uknowledge.uky.edu/cgi/viewcontent.cgi?article=1036&context=klj.

12 Ibid.

13 Victor Madrigal-Borloz, "Promotion and Protection of All Human Rights, Civil, Political, Economic, Social and Cultural Rights, Including the Right to Development," Human Rights Council, Fifty-Third session, June 19–July 14, 2023, Agenda item 3.

14 Ibid.

15 Dialectical Views, "Compilation of People Identifying as Weird Things," YouTube, September 30, 2022, https://www.youtube.com/watch?v=FUZHZqvuiLU.

Chapter 1: The Making of the Myth

1   Michael Joseph Gross, "Gay Is the New Black," *The Advocate*, December 2008, https://www.advocate.com/news/2008/11/16/gay-new-black.

2   Ibid.

3   NBC News, "Rachel Dolezal: 'I Definitely Am Not White'|NBC Nightly News," YouTube, June 17, 2015, https://www.youtube.com/watch?v=3B24Bbsf3U4.

4   Anthony Kennedy, *Obergefell v. Hodges*, Supreme Court of the United States, June 26, 2015, https://www.law.cornell.edu/supremecourt/text/14-556#writing-14-556_OPINION_3.

5   "Terminology," CDC Adolescent and School Health, last revewied December 23, 2022, https://www.cdc.gov/healthyyouth/terminology/sexual-and-gender-identity-terms.htm.

6 "Sexual and Gender Minority Populations," Association for Behavior and Cognitive Therapies, https://www.abct.org/fact-sheets/sexual-and-gender-minority-populations.

7 Ibid.

8 "Terminology," CDC Adolescent and School Health.

9 Postsecondary institutions within the United States conferred 3.1 million undergraduate degrees in 2020–21. These included one million associate degrees and 2.1 million bachelor degrees. The majority of both associate and bachelor degrees were conferred to female students. "Most Popular Majors," National Center for Education Statistics, retrieved May 16, 2023, https://nces.ed.gov/fastfacts/display.asp?id=37.

10 Ibid.

11 Veera Korhonen, "Total Population in the United States by Gender from 2010 to 2027," Statista, October 6, 2023, https://www.statista.com/statistics/737923/us-population-by-gender.

12 *Obergefell v. Hodges.*

13 Vishal Mangalwadi, *The Book That Made Your World: How the Bible Created the Soul of Western Civilization* (Nashville, Tennessee: Thomas Nelson, 2012). In his seminal work, Mangalwadi makes a compelling case for the biblical foundations of Western civilization. While he is not the only scholar to do so, he argues from the perspective of a culture that is not Western but has benefitted from Western civilization. As someone who has had the privilege of being born in America, living and studying for a season in the United Kingdom, and spending the last eight years in the global south, I found Mangalwadi's work very helpful.

Chapter 2: *Loving v. Virginia*

1 Supreme Court of the United States, *Loving v. Virginia*, June 12, 1967, http://law2.umkc.edu/faculty/projects/ftrials/conlaw/loving.html.

2 "What Is Modern Slavery?," Anti-Slavery International, https://www.antislavery.org/slavery-today/modern-slavery.

3 "During the Middle Ages, Slavs were so widely used as slaves in both Europe and the Islamic world that the very word 'slave' derived from the word for Slav—not only in English, but also in other European languages, as well as in Arabic." Thomas Sowell, *Black Rednecks and White Liberals* (New York: Encounter Books, 2006), 112.

4 Ibid., 113.

5 Ibid.

6 Ibid.

7   Ibid., 116.
8   Ibid., 127.
9   Ibid., 128.
10 Ibid.
11 The State's concern in these statutes, as expressed in the words of the 1924 bill's title, "An Act to Preserve Racial Integrity," extends only to the integrity of the white race. "While Virginia prohibits whites from marrying any nonwhite (subject to the exception for the descendants of Pocahontas), Negroes, Orientals, and any other racial class may intermarry without statutory interference." *Loving v. Virginia*, https://scholar .google.com/scholar_case?case=5103666188878568597&q=Loving +v.+Virginia&hl=en&as_sdt=2006.
12 Ibid.
13 Ibid.
14 Ibid.
15 Ibid.
16 Ibid.
17 We will deal with this claim later.
18 Ibid.
19 Ibid.
20 Ibid.
21 Ibid.
22 Many years have passed, so the words may not be exact. I have tried to get a copy of the transcript, without success. However, I wrote my recollection of the events in question very shortly after they occurred and have spoken of them often. I have also spoken with Dr. Shortt about the events many times over the years.

Chapter 3: The Founders of the Feast
1   For a helpful discussion of the broader ideological landscape and the names discussed here, see Carl R. Trueman, *The Rise and Triumph of the Modern Self* (Wheaton, Illinois: Crossway, 2020).
2   Alfred C. Kinsey, *Sexual Behavior in the Human Male* (Bloomington: Indiana University Press, 1948), 273.
3   Ibid.
4   Lillian Faderman, *The Gay Revolution: The Story of the Struggle* (New York: Simon & Schuster, 2015), 54.
5   Scott McLemee, "The Man Who Took Sex Out of the Closet," Salon, November 5, 1997, http://www.salon.com/books/feature/1997/11/cov _05kinsey.html.

6   E. Micháel Jones, *Libido Dominandi: Sexual Liberation and Political Control* (South Bend, Indiana: St. Augustine's Press, 2000), 571–72.
7   Ibid.
8   Kinsey, *Sexual Behavior in the Human Male*, 273.
9   Ibid.
10   Alex Newman, "The Sordid History and Deadly Consequences of 'Sex Ed' at School," *Epoch Times*, updated November 4, 2020, https://www.theepochtimes.com/opinion/the-sordid-history-and-deadly-consequences-of-sex-ed-at-school-3227274.
11   Judith Reisman, "Crafting Bi/Homosexual Youth," *Regent University Law Review* 14 (2001-2002): 283, https://www.regent.edu/acad/schlaw/student_life/studentorgs/lawreview/docs/issues/v14n2/Vol.%2014,%20No.%202,%204%20Reisman.pdf.
12   James H. Jones, *Alfred C. Kinsey: A Life* (New York: W. W. Norton & Company, 2004), 82.
13   Ibid., 604.
14   Ibid., 81.
15   Ibid.
16   Ibid., 606.
17   Ibid., 607.
18   Ibid.
19   Reisman, "Crafting Bi/Homosexual Youth," 313.
20   John Colapinto, *As Nature Made Him: The Boy Who Was Raised as a Girl* (New York: HarperCollins, 2006), 3.
21   Ibid., front matter.
22   Ibid., 159–60.
23   Ibid., loc. 72, Kindle.
24   Ibid., loc. 80, Kindle.
25   Ibid., 50.
26   Ibid., loc. 80, Kindle.
27   Laurel Duggan, "'We Were Wrong': Pioneer in Child Gender Dysphoria Treatment Says Trans Medical Industry Is Harming Kids," Daily Caller, March 12, 2023, https://dailycaller.com/2023/03/11/pioneer-in-child-gender-dysphoria-treatment-says-trans-medical-industry-is-harming-kids.
28   Colapinto, *As Nature Made Him*, loc. 87, Kindle.
29   Miriam Grossman, *You're Teaching My Child What?: A Physician Exposes the Lies of Sex Education and How They Harm Your Child* (Washington, D.C.: Regnery Publishing, 2023), 159.
30   Ibid., 161.
31   Colapinto, *As Nature Made Him*, 86.

32 Ibid., loc. 4, Kindle.
33 Jan Jekielek, "Dr. Miriam Grossman: How One Doctor's Lies Built the Gender Industry, Part I," *Epoch Times*, November 11, 2022, https://www.theepochtimes.com/audio/dr-miriam-grossman-how-one-doctors-lies-built-the-gender-industry-part-1_4852600.html.
34 Faderman, *The Gay Revolution*, 416.
35 Marshall Kirk and Hunter Madsen, *After the Ball: How America Will Conquer Its Fear and Hatred of Gays in the 90's* (New York: Doubleday, 1989), xxv.
36 Ibid., 14.
37 Ibid.
38 Ibid., 15
39 Ibid., xxvi.
40 Ibid., 162–3.
41 Ibid., 149.
42 Ibid., 178.
43 Reisman, "Crafting Bi/Homosexual Youth," 283.
44 "259 LGBTQ Characters in Cartoons That Bust the Myth That Kids Can't Handle Inclusion," Business Insider, https://www.insider.com/lgbtq-cartoon-characters-kids-database-2021-06?page=explore-database.
45 Abigail Shrier, *Irreversible Damage: The Transgender Craze Seducing Our Daughters* (Washington, D.C.: Regnery Publishing, 2021), 66.
46 Ibid., 69.
47 Jeff Horseman, "Gov. Gavin Newsom Says State Will Provide Social Studies Textbooks to Temecula If School Board Won't," *Mercury News*, July 14, 2023, https://www.mercurynews.com/2023/07/14/gov-gavin-newsom-says-state-will-provide-temecula-textbooks-if-school-board-wont.
48 Kirk and Madsen, *After the Ball*, 179.
49 Ibid., 151–2.
50 Patrick Letellier and David Island, *Men Who Beat the Men Who Love Them: Battered Gay Men and Domestic Violence* (New York: Harrington Park Press, 1991), 16.
51 Ibid.
52 Ibid., 14.
53 Kirk and Madsen, *After the Ball*, 153–4.
54 Ibid.
55 Ibid.
56 Steve Warren, "Warning to Homophobes," *The Advocate*, September 1987.

Chapter 4: The Ubiquitous, Ever-Growing, Self-Contradictory Acronym—Part I: LGBT

1   LGBTQ Nation, "What Is the Progress Pride Flag?," updated July 26, 2022, https://www.lgbtqnation.com/2022/06/progress-pride-flag.

2   Faderman, *The Gay Revolution*, 77.

3   Ibid.

4   Kirk and Madsen, *After the Ball*, 184.

5   Michael Brown, *A Queer Thing Happened to America: And What a Long, Strange Trip It's Been* (BookMasters), 1, citing "Empowering Parents of Gender Discordant and Same-Sex Attracted Children," accessed December 14, 2010, http://www.americancollegeofpedia tricians.org/Download-document/8-Empowering-Parents-of-Gender -Discordant-and-Same-Sex-Attracted-Children.html. This link has since been removed from the organization's website.

6   Ian Oxnevad, "Professor's Redefinition of Pedophilia Could Help Offenders Demand Rights," *New York Post*, https://nypost.com/2022 /01/01/professors-redefinition-of-pedophilia-could-help-offenders -demand-rights.

7   Lisa M. Diamond, *Sexual Fluidity: Understanding Women's Love and Desire* (Cambridge, Massachusetts: Harvard University Press, 2009), 110. Cited by Grossman, *You're Teaching My Child What?*, 227.

8   Ibid., 147.

9   Ibid., 153.

10 Ibid., 153–5.

11 Ibid.

12 Ibid.

13 *Merriam-Webster*, s.v. "Bisexual," https://www.merriam-webster.com /dictionary/bisexuals.

14 Gabrielle Kassel, "How Do You Know If You're Bisexual?," Healthline, January 14, 2021, https://www.healthline.com/health/am-i-bisexual #how-to-tell.

15 Jeffrey M. Jones, "LGBT Identification in U.S. Ticks Up to 7.1%," Gallup, February 17, 2022, https://news.gallup.com/poll/389792/lgbt -identification-ticks-up.aspx.

16 Ibid.

17 Kendall Tietz, "Over 100 Gender, Sexuality Options on Application for San Francisco's Guaranteed Transgender Income Program," FoxNews.com, November 19, 2022, https://www.foxnews.com/media /over-100-gender-sexuality-options-application-san-franciscos -guaranteed-transgender-income-program.

18 Grossman, *You're Teaching My Child What?*, 168–69.

19 "Caitlyn Jenner Vows to 'Reshape the Landscape' in ESPYS Speech," ESPN, July 15, 2015, https://www.espn.com/espys/2015/story/_/id /13264599/caitlyn-jenner-accepts-arthur-ashe-courage-award-espys -ashe2015.

20 Will Mendelson, "Caitlyn Jenner at Women of the Year Awards: I Never in a Million Years Thought I'd Be Here," *US Weekly*, November 10, 2015, https://www.usmagazine.com/celebrity-news /news/caitlyn-jenner-at-women-of-the-year-awards-never-thought-id -be-here-20151011.

21 Amanda Musa, "Transgender Swimmer Lia Thomas Nominated for NCAA 2022 Woman of the Year Award," CNN.com, July 15, 2022, https://edition.cnn.com/2022/07/15/sport/lia-thomas-ncaa-woman -of-the-year-nomination/index.html.

22 Doha Madani and Julie Tsirkin, "Dr. Rachel Levine Becomes First Openly Transgender Person Confirmed by Senate to Federal Post," NBC News, March 24, 2021, https://www.nbcnews.com/politics /congress/dr-rachel-levine-becomes-first-openly-transgender-person -confirmed-senate-n1262000.

23 Myah Ward, "Blackburn to Jackson: Can You Define 'the Word Woman'?" Politico, March 22, 2022, https://www.politico.com/news/2022/03 /22/blackburn-jackson-define-the-word-woman-00019543.

24 Shrier, *Irreversible Damage*, 69.

25 Ibid.

26 Ibid., 70.

27 Ibid., 70–1.

28 Grossman, *You're Teaching My Child What?*, 15–16.

29 Shrier, *Irreversible Damage*, 60.

30 Ibid., 63.

31 Ibid., 64.

32 Marianne J. Legato, "The International Society for Gender Medicine: History and Highlights," Foundation for Gender-Specific Medicine, July 25, 2019, https://gendermed.org/the-international-society-for-gender -medicine-history-and-highlights.

33 Grossman, *You're Teaching My Child What?*, 181.

34 Ibid.

Chapter 5: The Ubiquitous, Ever-Growing, Self-Contradicting Acronym—Part II: QIA2S+

1   Carl R. Trueman, *The Rise and Triumph of the Modern Self* (Wheaton, Illinois: Crossway Books), 380.

2   Helen Pluckrose and James A. Lindsay, *Cynical Theories: How Activist Scholarship Made Everything about Race, Gender, and Identity—and Why This Harms Everybody* (Durham, North Carolina: Pitchstone Publishing, 2020), 89.

3   Ibid.

4   Hannah Dyer, "Queer Futurity and Childhood Innocence: Beyond the Injury of Development," *Global Studies of Childhood* 7, no. 3 (2017): 293, https://journals.sagepub.com/doi/full/10.1177/2043610616671056.

5   Ben Appel, "The New Homophobia," *Newsweek*, April 21, 2022, https://www.newsweek.com/new-homophobia-opinion-1698969.

6   Ibid.

7   "What Is Drag Story Hour?," Drag Story Hour (formerly Drag Queen Story Hour), https://www.dragstoryhour.org/about.

8   Christopher F. Rufo, "The War on Innocence," Substack, March 16, 2022, https://christopherrufo.com/the-war-on-innocence/?mc_cid=569a7c5199&mc_eid=89e2024f5a.

9   Ibid.

10 Ibid.

11 Christopher F. Rufo, "Radical Gender Lessons for Young Children," Substack, April 21, 2022, https://christopherrufo.com/radical-gender-lessons-for-young-children/?mc_cid=569a7c5199&mc_eid=89e2024f5a.

12 Ibid.

13 Ibid.

14 Christopher F. Rufo, "Sexual Liberation in Public Schools," Substack July 20, 2022, https://christopherrufo.com/sexual-liberation-in-public-schools/?mc_cid=569a7c5199&mc_eid=89e2024f5a.

15 Ibid.

16 Christopher F. Rufo, "Sexual Disturbance," Substack, September 21, 2022, https://rufo.substack.com/p/secual-disturbance?utm_source=%2Fsearch%2FSexual%2520Disturbance&utm_medium=reader2.

17 Ibid.

18 Ibid.

19 Ibid.

20 Miriam Grossman, *You're Teaching My Child What?: A Physician Exposes the Lies of Sex Education and How They Harm Your Child* (Washington, D.C.: Regnery Publishing, 2023), 15–16.

21 Gayle S. Rubin, "Thinking Sex: Notes for a Radical Theory of the Politics of Sexuality," reprinted in *The Gay and Lesbian Studies*

Reader (New York: Rutledge, 1993), 154, http://www.faculty.umb
.edu/heike.schotten/readings/Rubin,%20Thinking%20Sex.pdf.
22 Ibid.
23 Ibid., 147.
24 Ibid.
25 Ibid.
26 Ibid., 148.
27 Ibid., 149.
28 Dyer, "Queer Futurity and Childhood Innocence," 290–302.
29 Ibid.
30 Ibid., 291.
31 Ibid., 293.
32 Ibid., 291.
33 Ibid., 291–92.
34 Ibid., 291.
35 Ibid., 292.
36 Ibid.
37 Debra Soh, *The End of Gender: Debunking the Myths about Sex and Identity in Our Society* (New York: Threshold Editions, 2020), 23. For example, girls with an intersex condition called androgen insensitivity syndrome have XY chromosomes and male internal organs, but their body can't respond to testosterone, so they will appear female. And some intersex people have chromosomes that are typical of their sex. For instance, girls with congenital adrenal hyperplasia, another intersex condition, experience masculinization in the womb and have XX chromosomes typical of females.
38 Ibid.
39 Ibid.
40 Dictionary.com, s.v. "two-spirit," January 26, 2021, https://www.dictionary.com/e/gender-sexuality/two-spirit.
41 Simon J. Kistemaker, *Exposition of the Acts of the Apostles* (Grand Rapids: Baker Academic, 1990), 631.
42 Stephen Baskerville, *The New Politics of Sex: The Sexual Revolution, Civil Liberties, and the Growth of Governmental Power* (Kettering, Ohio: Angelico Press, 2017), 13–14.

Chapter 6: How We Got Here
1   Rev. Osagyefo Uhuru Sekou, "Gays Are the New Niggers," Killing the Buddha, June 26, 2009, https://killingthebuddha.com/mag/damnation/gays-are-the-new-niggers.

2   John D'Emilio, *Lost Prophet: The Life and Times of Bayard Rustin* (Chicago, Illinois: Free Press, 2004), 231.

3   Samantha Schmidt, "Arrested for Having Sex with Men, This Gay Civil Rights Leader Could Finally Be Pardoned in California," *Washington Post*, January 21, 2020, https://www.washingtonpost.com/history/2020/01/21/bayard-rustin-gay-pardon.

4   Lillian Faderman, *The Gay Revolution: The Story of the Struggle* (New York: Simon & Schuster, 2015), 416.

5   Marshall Kirk and Hunter Madsen, *After the Ball: How America Will Conquer Its Fear and Hatred of Gays in the 90's* (New York: Doubleday, 1989), xxv.

6   "Romney Statement on the Respect for Marriage Act," Mitt Romney, U.S. Senator for Utah, November 16, 2022, https://www.romney.senate.gov/romney-statement-on-the-respect-for-marriage-act.

7   Ibid.

8   Cyd Zeigler, "Drag Queen, LGBT Fans Star alongside Serene Williams and Ukraine in New ESPN Ad," OutSports, October 26, 2022, https://www.outsports.com/2022/10/26/23423275/espn-seat-for-everyone-ad-serena-ukraine-lgbt-drag-queen.

9   Wikipedia, s.v. "List of Dramatic Television Series with LGBT Characters: 2020s," https://en.wikipedia.org/wiki/List_of_dramatic_television_series_with_LGBT_characters:_2020s.

10 OWN, "Pastor Joel Osteen Discusses Sin and the Path to God|Oprah's Next Chapter|Oprah Winfrey Network," YouTube, January 8, 2012, https://youtu.be/7XXUfTNCkzc.

11 CNN, "CNN Official Interview: Joel Osteen 'Homosexuality Is a Sin,'" YouTube, January 25, 2011, https://youtu.be/tgCpRNfBzys.

12 Bydesign001, "'Being Gay Is a Sin: Joel Osteen Ambushed by Soledad O'Brien, Richard Socarides, CNN 09202012," YouTube, September 23, 2012, https://youtu.be/qOG7-PYqNvU.

13 Tom Manning, "Carl Lentz with Katie Couric 12:14," YouTube, June 4, 2014, https://youtu.be/_3wLm6pPvRY.

14 HuffPost Live, "Bishop T. D. Jakes on the Black Church's Shifting Stance on Homosexuality," YouTube, August 11, 2015, https://youtu.be/F5MRhqSK8Ts.

15 Aliyah Frumin, "Timeline: Bill Clinton's Evolution on Gay Rights," MSNBC, March 8, 2013, https://www.msnbc.com/hardball/timeline-bill-clintons-evolution-gay-rig-msna19626.

16 Tracy Baim, "Obama Changed Views on Gay Marriage," *Windy City Times*, January 14, 2009, https://windycitytimes.com/images/publications/wct/2009-01-14/current.pdf.

17 Zeke J. Miller, "Obama Says He Didn't Mislead on Gay Marriage," *TIME*, February 11, 2015, https://time.com/3704760/barack-obama-gay-marriage-david-axelrod; TeaPartySanDiego, "Obama's Lies: I Believe Marriage Is between a Man and a Woman," YouTube, February 7, 2013, https://www.youtube.com/watch?v=S5L2LMJcRIg.

18 "Transcript: Robin Roberts ABC News Interview with President Obama," ABC News, May 9, 2012, https://abcnews.go.com/Politics/transcript-robin-roberts-abc-news-interview-president-obama/story?id=16316043.

19 "Obama Makes History by Citing Gay Rights in Inaugural Address," ABC News, January 21, 2013, https://abcnews.go.com/Politics/obama-makes-history-citing-gay-rights-inaugural-address/story?id=18275341.

20 "Transcript for June 4: Joseph Biden, Hans Blix, Jon Harwood, Glen Ifill," NBC News, June 4, 2006, https://www.nbcnews.com/id/wbna13085904#.XvDtOxNKg8c.

21 Adam Nagourney and Thomas Kaplan, "Behind Joe Biden's Evolution on L.G.B.T.Q. Rights," *New York Times*, June 21, 2020, https://www.nytimes.com/2020/06/21/us/politics/biden-gay-rights-lgbt.html.

22 Editorial Staff, "2006 Clip of Joe Biden's Opposition to Gay Marriage Surfaces," 93.1 FM WIBC, July 22, 2020, https://wibc.com/90041/2006-clip-of-joe-bidens-opposition-to-gay-marriage-surfaces.

23 Nagourney and Kaplan, "Behind Joe Biden's Evolution on L.G.B.T.Q. Rights."

24 Ibid.

25 "Statement from President Joe Biden on the Enactment of Uganda's Anti-Homosexuality Act," The White House, May 29, 2023, https://www.whitehouse.gov/briefing-room/statements-releases/2023/05/29/statement-from-president-joe-biden-on-the-enactment-of-ugandas-anti-homosexuality-act.

26 Andrew Mark Miller, "Melania Slams 'Establishment Enemies' Calling Trump Anti-Gay: 'Nothing Could Be Further from the Truth,'" *Washington Examiner*, October 30, 2020, https://www.washingtonexaminer.com/news/melania-slams-establishment-enemies-calling-trump-anti-gay-nothing-could-be-further-from-the-truth.

27 "Trump Is for Traditional Marriage," CNN, June 28, 2015, https://edition.cnn.com/videos/politics/2015/06/28/sotu-tapper-trump-is-for-traditional-marriage.cnn.

28 "Donald Trump Punching Back," Fox News, updated January 26, 2017, https://www.foxnews.com/transcript/donald-trump-punching-back.

29 Janice Min, "The Donald Trump Conversation: Murdoch, Ailes, NBC and the Rush of Being TV's 'Ratings Machine,'" *Hollywood Reporter*, August 19, 2015, https://www.hollywoodreporter.com/news/politics-news/donald-trump-murdoch-ailes-nbc-816131.

30 "Ted Cruz Attacks Donald Trump's Financial Record; Trump Responds," Fox News, January 31, 2016, https://www.foxnews.com/transcript/ted-cruz-attacks-donald-trumps-financial-record-trump-responds.

31 Log Cabin Republicans (@LogCabinGOP), "President @realDonald Trump made history for #LGBT Americans . . . ," Twitter, August 19, 2020, 7:00 a.m., https://twitter.com/LogCabinGOP/status/1296039209891819520?s=20.

32 Jerome Hudson, *50 Things They Don't Want You to Know* (New York: Broadside, 2019), 40.

33 Ibid., 43.

34 Miller, "Melania Slams 'Establishment Enemies' Calling Trump Anti-Gay."

35 Hudson, *50 Things They Don't Want You to Know*, 43.

36 Meridith McGraw, "The GOP Waves White Flag in the Same-Sex Marriage Wars," Politico, August 16, 2021, https://www.politico.com/news/2021/08/16/republicans-gay-marriage-wars-505041.

Chapter 7: The Enemy Within

1   Mastin Kipp, "Why Jesus Loves LGBT People and Gay Marriage Doesn't Exist," Huffpost, July 31, 2012, updated September 30, 2012, https://www.huffpost.com/entry/why-jesus-loves-lgbt-people-and-gay-marriage-doesnt-exist_b_1713871.

2   Ibid.

3   Ibid.

4   Ibid.

5   Ibid., 1–2.

6   Ibid.

7   Marcia Ledford, "What Is Political Theology?," Political Theology Matters, https://www.politicaltheologymatters.com.

8   Ibid.

9   Marcia Ledford, "What Are the Clobber Passages? Stop Shaming LGBTQ People with the Bible," Political Theology Matters, September 1, 2021, https://www.politicaltheologymatters.com/what-are-the-clobber-passages/.

10 Ibid.

11 Ibid.

12 Ibid.

13 Matthew Vines, *God and the Gay Christian: The Biblical Case in Support of Same-Sex Relationships* (New York: Convergent Books, 2015), 36.

14 "US Troops Taught Sexual Abuse Was 'Culturally Accepted Practice' in Afghanistan," RT, November 17, 2017, https://www.rt.com/usa/410206-pentagon-afghanistan-sexual-abuse.

15 Joel Brinkley, "Afghanistan's Dirty Little Secret," SFGate, August 29, 2010, https://www.sfgate.com/opinion/brinkley/article/afghanistan-s-dirty-little-secret-3176762.php.

16 Dwight Longenecker, "Man Boy Sex in Afghanistan," Patheos, last updated December 27, 2014, https://www.patheos.com/blogs/standingonmyhead/2013/11/man-boy-sex-in-afghanistan.html.

17 Vines, *God and the Gay Christian*, 11–12.

18 Ibid., 15.

19 *The West Wing*, season 2, episode 3, "The Midterms," directed by Alex Graves, written by Aaron Sorkin, aired October 18, 2000 on NBC.

20 "Blackstone's Commentaries on the Laws of England, Introduction," Yale Law School, https://avalon.law.yale.edu/18th_century/blackstone_intro.asp#2.

21 Ibid.

Chapter 8: Is It Fair to Use the Bible?

1   Allan Bloom, *The Closing of the American Mind: How Higher Education Has Failed Democracy and Impoverished the Souls of Today's Students* (New York: Simon & Schuster, 1987), 58.

2   "Environmental Public Health Inspection Report: Grace Life Church of Edmonton," Alberta Health Services, February 2, 2021, https://www.jccf.ca/wp-content/uploads/2021/02/2021-Feb-14-Grace-Life-Church-AHS-Inspection-Report.pdf.

3   Alejandra Molina, "John MacArthur's Church to Receive $800K COVID-19 Settlement," *Christianity Today*, September 21, 2021, https://www.christianitytoday.com/news/2021/september/john-macarthur-covid-settlement-california-church-grace-com.html.

4   Ibid.

5   William Hendriksen, *Exposition of Paul's Epistle to the Romans* (Grand Rapids: Baker Book House, 1981), xii–xiii, 433.

6   John Calvin, *Commentary on the Epistle of Paul the Apostle to the Romans* (Bellingham, Washington: Logos Bible Software, 2010), 478.

7   Robert H. Mounce, *The New American Commentary: Romans* (Nashville, Tennessee: Broadman & Holman Publishers, 1995), xxvii, 243.

8   Charles Simeon, *Horae Homileticae: Romans* (London: Holdsworth and Ball, 1833), xv.

9   Ibid., 505.

10   "Declaration of Independence: A Transcription," National Archives, https://www.archives.gov/founding-docs/declaration-transcript.

11   Ibid.

12   Martin Luther King Jr., "I Have a Dream," delivered August 28, 1963, American Rhetoric, https://www.americanrhetoric.com/speeches /mlkihaveadream.htm.

13   Ibid.

14   Calvin, *Commentary on the Epistle of Paul the Apostle to the Romans*, 481.

15   D. A. Carson, R. T. France, J. A. Motyer, and G. J. Wenham, eds., "Romans," in *New Bible Commentary: 21st Century Edition* (Leicester, England: Inter-Varsity Press, 1994), 1152.

16   Matthew J. Trewhella, *The Doctrine of the Lesser Magistrates: A Proper Resistance to Tyranny and a Repudiation of Unlimited Obedience to Civil Government* (self-pub., CreateSpace, 2013), 2.

17   Ibid., 105.

18   Ibid., 3.

19   Lillian Faderman, *The Gay Revolution: The Story of the Struggle* (New York: Simon & Schuster, 2015), 604.

Chapter 9: What Happens When We Buy the Lie?

1   Stanley Kurtz, "Beyond Gay Marriage," *Weekly Standard*, August 4, 2003, https://pages.pomona.edu/~vis04747/h21/readings/Kurz_Beyond _gay_marriage.pdf.

2   Felicia R. Lee, "'Big Love': Real Polygamists Look at HBO Polygamists and Find Sex," *New York Times*, March 28, 2006, https://www .nytimes.com/2006/03/28/arts/television/big-love-real-polygamists -look-at-hbo-polygamists-and-find.html.

3   Ibid.

4   "Iowa Supreme Court Case Varnum v. Brien, April 3, 2009," State Historical Society of Iowa, https://history.iowa.gov/history/education /educator-resources/primary-source-sets/government-democracy -and-laws/varnum.

5   Good Morning Britain, "Gender-Neutral Family Are Raising Their Child as a 'Theyby,' | Good Morning Britain," YouTube, March 12, 2019, https://www.youtube.com/watch?v=S1pW6r9kjiw.

6   Derek McCullough and David S. Hall, "Polyamory: What It Is and What It Isn't," *Electronic Journal of Human Sexuality* 6 (February 27, 2003), http://www.ejhs.org/volume6/polyamory.htm.

7   Elizabeth Emens, "Monogamy's Law: Compulsory Monogamy and Polyamorous Existence" (working paper, Public Law and Legal Theory Working Papers, University of Chicago Law School, 2004), https://chicagounbound.uchicago.edu/cgi/viewcontent.cgi?article=1193&context=public_law_and_legal_theory.

8   Ibid.

9   "Beyond Same-Sex Marriage: A New Strategic Vision for All Our Families and Relationships," *Studies in Gender and Sexuality* 9, no. 2 (2008): 161–71, https://doi.org/10.1080/15240650801935198.

10   Jack Drescher, "Out of DSM: Depathologizing Homosexuality," *Behavioral Sciences* 5, no. 4 (2015):565–675, https://www.ncbi.nlm.nih.gov/pmc/articles/PMC4695779.

11   Ray Levy Uyeda, "How LGBTQ+ Activists Got 'Homosexuality' out of the DSM," JSTOR Daily, May 26, 2021, https://daily.jstor.org/how-lgbtq-activists-got-homosexuality-out-of-the-dsm.

12   Ibid.

13   Ibid.

14   Hope Gillette, "Pedophilic Disorder Symptoms," PsychCentral, updated July 30, 2021, https://psychcentral.com/disorders/pedophilic-disorder-symptoms#what-is-it.

15   Ian Oxnevad, "Professor's Redefinition of Pedophilia Could Help Offenders Demand Rights," *New York Post*, January 1, 2022, https://nypost.com/2022/01/01/professors-redefinition-of-pedophilia-could-help-offenders-demand-rights.

16   He-Meme Man, "Stephen Kershnar Argues in Favor of Pedophilia," YouTube, August 28, 2022, https://www.youtube.com/watch?v=Zc-jZkwsEm8k. See also Kendall Tietz, "Liberal Professor Defends Wanting to Have Sex With a 12-Year-Old," LifeNews, February 2, 2022, https://www.lifenews.com/2022/02/02/liberal-professor-defends-wanting-to-have-sex-with-a-12-year-old. The original videos have been removed from Libs of TikTok.

17   "1977 French Petition against Age of Consent Laws," Internet Archives, https://archive.org/details/letter-scanned-and-ocr.

18   Matthew Campbell, "French Philosopher Michel Foucault 'Abused Boys in Tunisia,'" *The Sunday Times*, March 28, 2021, https://www

.thetimes.co.uk/article/french-philosopher-michel-foucault-abused
-boys-in-tunisia-6t5sj7jvw.

19 Jackie Salo, "Transgender Woman Wins Miss Nevada USA Pageant,
Making History," *New York Post*, June 29, 2021, https://nypost
.com/2021/06/29/transgender-woman-wins-miss-nevada-usa
-pageant-making-history.

20 Madeline Leesman, "Transgender Biological Male Wins Local 'Miss
America' Beauty Pageant," Townhall, November 10, 2022, https:
//townhall.com/tipsheet/madelineleesman/2022/11/10/transgender
-biological-male-wins-local-miss-america-beauty-pageant
-n2615804#google_vignette.

21 Taylor Gold, "For 1st Time in 99 Years, California Crowns
Transgender Woman in Beauty Pageant," MSN, https://www.msn
.com/en-us/lifestyle/lifestyle-buzz/for-1st-time-in-99-years-california
-crowns-transgender-woman-in-beauty-pageant/ar-AA1eyvZi.

22 Emma Green, "The Culture War over 'Pregnant People'," *The Atlantic*,
September 17, 2021, https://www.theatlantic.com/politics/archive/2021
/09/pregnant-people-gender-identity/620031.

23 Matthew Schmitz, "How Gay Marriage Changed America," *First
Things*, April 2023, https://www.firstthings.com/article/2023/04/how
-gay-marriage-changed-america.

24 Ibid.

25 Ibid.

26 "Begging the Question," Fallacy Files, http://www.fallacyfiles.org/begquest
.html.

27 Ibid.

28 Quote by William F. Buckley Jr., AZ Quotes, https://www.azquotes.
com/quote/1444689.

29 Michael K. Lavers, "NAACP President: Marriage Is 'Civil Rights
Issue of Our Times,'" *Washington Blade*, May 12, 2012, https:
//www.washingtonblade.com/2012/05/21/naacp-president-marriage
-is-civil-rights-issue-of-our-times.

30 Lisa DePaulo, "The Reconstructionist," *GQ*, March 11, 2009, https:
//www.gq.com/story/-the-reconstructionist-michael-steele.

31 Benjamin Brink, "Portland Mayor Sam Adams Apologizes for 'Sexual
Relationship' with Teenager," *The Oregonian*, January 20, 2009,
https://www.oregonlive.com/portland/2009/01/portland_mayor
_sam_adams_press.html.

32 Antonin Scalia, "*John Geddes Lawrence and Tyron Garner, Petitioners
v. Texas*," 539 U.S., ed. Supreme Court of the United States, June 26,
2003, https://www.oyez.org/cases/2002/02-102.

33 Antonin Scalia, "Dissent, *Obergefell v. Hodges*," Supreme Court of the United States, June 26, 2015, https://www.law.cornell.edu/supremecourt/text/14-556#writing-14-556_DISSENT_5.

Chapter 10: God's Design for Marriage

1   Debra Soh, *The End of Gender: Debunking the Myths about Sex and Identity in Our Society* (New York: Threshold Editions, 2020), 221.

2   Matthew Vines, *God and the Gay Christian: The Biblical Case in Support of Same-Sex Relationships* (New York: Convergent Books, 2015), 45.

3   John D. Currid, "A Study Commentary on Genesis: Genesis 1:1–25:18," in *EP Study Commentary* (Darlington, England: Evangelical Press, 2015), i, 109.

4   Joseph Haroutunian and Louise Pettibone Smith, *Calvin: Commentaries* (Philadelphia: Westminster Press, 1958), 357.

5   Ibid.

6   Currid, "A Study Commentary on Genesis: Genesis 1:1–25:18," i, 142.

7   Rosaria Champagne Butterfield, *The Secret Thoughts of an Unlikely Convert: An English Professor's Journey into Christian Faith* (Pittsburgh: Crown & Covenant Publications, 2012), 96.

8   Ibid.

9   Ibid., 108.

10 Ibid.

11 Eugene E. Carpenter and Philip W. Comfort, *Holman Treasury of Key Bible Words: 200 Greek and 200 Hebrew Words Defined and Explained* (Nashville, Tennessee: Broadman & Holman Publishers, 2000), 385.

12 Vines, *God and the Gay Christian*, 12.

13 Surgeon General C. Everett Koop, quoted in Miriam Grossman, *You're Teaching My Child What?: A Physician Exposes the Lies of Sex Education and How They Harm Your Child* (Washington, D.C.: Regnery Publishing, 2023), 91.

14 Ibid., 86–87.

15 "Condoms and Sexually Transmitted Diseases, Brochure," U.S. Food and Drug Administration, December 1990.

16 Grossman, *You're Teaching My Child What?*, 89–90.

17 "Condoms and Sexually Transmitted Diseases, Brochure," U.S. Food and Drug Administration, December 1990. Jacobs utilized this brochure, which is no longer available on the internet, while working in tandem with Citizens for a Responsible Curriculum to present

Montgomery County Public Schools with a list of demands for the board to stop giving children misleading information about the efficacy of condoms and the risk of disease through its promotion of anal sex.

18 Hui Zhang Kudon et al., "Trends in Condomless Sex among MSM Who Participated in CDC-Funded HIV Risk-Reduction Interventions in the United States, 2012–2017," *Journal of Public Health Management and Practice* 28, no. 2 (March–April 2022): 170–3.

19 Grossman, *You're Teaching My Child What?*, 100.

20 Sara Nelson Glick et al., "A Comparison of Sexual Behavior Patterns among Men Who Have Sex with Men and Heterosexual Men and Women," *Journal of Acquired Immune Deficiency Syndromes* 60, no. 1 (May 2012): 83–90, https://www.ncbi.nlm.nih.gov/pmc/articles /PMC3334840/.

21 Alayne D. Markland et al., "Anal Intercourse and Fecal Incontinence: Evidence from the 2009–2010 National Health and Nutrition Examination Survey," *American Journal of Gastroenterology* 111, no. 2 (February 2016): 269–74, https://pubmed.ncbi.nlm.nih.gov /26753893.

Chapter 11: And Such Were Some of You

1 Rosaria Champagne Butterfield, *The Secret Thoughts of an Unlikely Convert: An English Professor's Journey into Christian Faith* (Pittsburgh: Crown & Covenant Publications, 2012), 2.

2 Ibid.

3 BJU Seminary, "Rosaria Butterfield's Testimony," YouTube, February 19, 2019, https://www.youtube.com/watch?v=Eykv-3hvFvI.

4 Ibid.

5 Ibid.

6 Ibid.

7 Ibid.

8 Ibid.

9 Ibid.

10 Christopher Yuan, *Holy Sexuality and the Gospel: Sex, Desire, and Relationships* (New York: Multnomah, 2018). Also see Christopher Yuan's interview on *The Sword and the Trowel*, available at https://founders.org/podcasts/tstt-christopher-yuan-holy-sexuality -and-the-gospel-sex-desire-relationships.

11 Ibid.

12 Ibid.

13 Ibid.

14 Ibid.

15 Ibid.

16 Ibid.

17 Ibid.

18 Ibid.

19 Ibid.

20 Ibid.

21 Ibid.

22 Ibid.

23 Matthew Vines, *God and the Gay Christian: The Biblical Case in Support of Same-Sex Relationships* (New York: Convergent Books, 2015), 10.

24 Ibid.

25 Ibid.

26 Ibid., 18.

27 Ibid.

28 Ibid.

29 Greg Johnson, "I Used to Hide My Shame. Now I Take Shelter under the Gospel," *Christianity Today*, May 20, 2019, https://www .christianitytoday.com/ct/2019/may-web-only/greg-johnson-hide -shame-shelter-gospel-gay-teenager.html.

30 Ibid.

31 Robert L. Spitzer, "Can Some Gay Men and Lesbians Change Their Sexual Orientation? 200 Participants Reporting a Change from Homosexual to Heterosexual Orientation," *Archives of Sexual Behavior* 32, no. 5 (October 2003): 403–17, https://doi.org/10.1023/A:1025 647527010.

32 Ibid.

33 Alfred C. Kinsey, *Sexual Behavior in the Human Male* (Bloomington: Indiana University Press, 1948), 948–9.

34 Vines, *God and the Gay Christian*, 170–1.

35 M. Price, "Genes Matter in Addiction," *Monitor on Psychology* 39, no. 6 (June 2008), https://www.apa.org/monitor/2008/06/genes-addict.

36 Sara Reardon, "Massive Study Finds No Single Genetic Cause of Same-Sex Sexual Behavior," *Scientific American*, August 29, 2019, https://www.scientificamerican.com/article/massive-study-finds-no -single-genetic-cause-of-same-sex-sexual-behavior.

37 Lance and Zachary Dodes, *The Sober Truth: Debunking the Bad Science behind 12-Step Programs and the Rehab Industry* (Boston: Beacon Press, 2014), 19.

38 Ibid.

39 Ibid., 56.
40 "Bill C-4: An Act to Amend the Criminal Code (Conversion Therapy)," Government of Canada, November 27, 2023, https://www.justice .gc.ca/eng/csj-sjc/pl/charter-charte/c4_1.html.
41 Substance Abuse and Mental Health Services Administration, "Lesbian, Gay, and Bisexual Behavioral Health: Results from the 2021 and 2022 National Surveys on Drug Use and Health," Center for Behavioral Health Statistics and Quality, Substance Abuse, and Mental Health Services Administration, June 2023, https://www .samhsa.gov/data/sites/default/files/reports/rpt41899/2022_LGB _Brief_Final_06_07_23.pdf. See also Hudaisa Hafeez et al., "Health Care Disparities among Lesbian, Gay, Bisexual, and Transgender Youth: A Literature Review," *Cureus* 9, no. 4 (April 2017), https: //www.ncbi.nlm.nih.gov/pmc/articles/PMC5478215.
42 Dodes, *The Sober Truth*, 134.
43 Butterfield, *The Secret Thoughts of an Unlikely Convert*, 83.
44 Ibid.

Conclusion

1   SFGMC TV, "'A Message from the Gay Community' Performed by the San Francisco Gay Men's Chorus," YouTube, July 1, 2021, https: //www.youtube.com/watch?v=ArOQF4kadHA.
2   Dr. Martin Luther King, Jr., "I Have a Dream," American Rhetoric, https://www.americanrhetoric.com/speeches/mlkihaveadream.htm.